Freshwater Fishes of Texas

RIVER BOOKS
Sponsored by

 the River Systems Institute
at Texas State University

Andrew Sansom,
General Editor

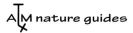

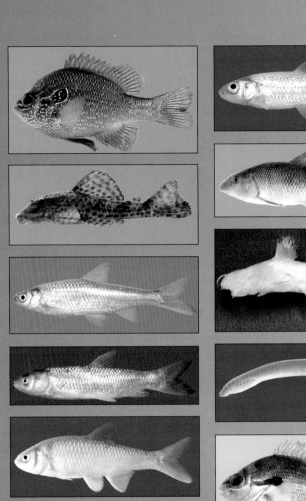
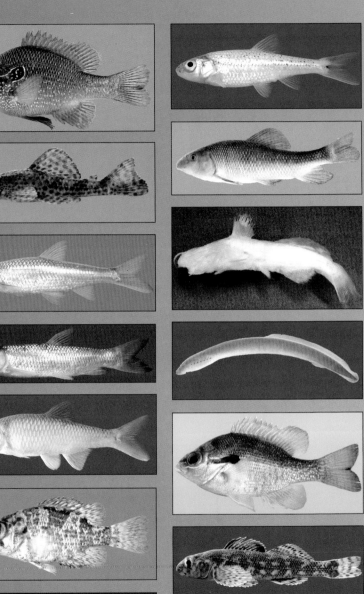

Freshwater Fishes of Texas

A FIELD GUIDE

Chad Thomas,
Timothy H. Bonner
& Bobby G. Whiteside

Foreword by Fran Gelwick

TEXAS A&M UNIVERSITY PRESS
COLLEGE STATION

Photographs are by Chad Thomas.

LIBRARY OF CONGRESS CATALOGING-IN-PUBLICATION DATA

Thomas, Chad, 1970–
    Freshwater fishes of Texas : a field guide / Chad Thomas,
Timothy H. Bonner, and Bobby G. Whiteside.—1st ed.
        p. cm.—(River books)
    Includes bibliographical references and index.
    ISBN-13: 978-1-58544-570-7 (flexbound : alk. paper)
    ISBN-10: 1-58544-570-3 (flexbound : alk. paper)
    1. Freshwater fishes—Texas—Identification.
2. Freshwater fishes—Texas—Pictorial works.
I. Bonner, Timothy H. (Timothy Hallman), 1969–
II. Whiteside, Bobby G., 1940–   III. Title.
QL628.T4T46   2007
597.17609764—dc22   2006029777

Contents

Series Editor's Preface

As I sit at my computer and gaze into the headwaters of the San Marcos River through my office window, I feel a deep sense of privilege at being a part of the family here at Texas State University–San Marcos. Perhaps because the university is home to the magnificent springs that give birth to one of Texas' most beautiful and diverse watercourses, it is also home to one of the finest aquatic biology programs of any university in all of North America. No better proof of that could exist than the collaboration of three academic generations to produce *Freshwater Fishes of Texas: A Field Guide,* written by Chad Thomas, his major professor Tim Bonner, and Bonner's major professor, Bobby Whiteside.

The timing of this book—the most comprehensive publication to date on the extraordinary diversity of our native fish species—could not be more critical, as Texas strives to finally come to grips with the in-stream flow needs of its rivers and streams to protect the richness of their aquatic biodiversity, including their fishes. The future of the freshwater fishes portrayed on these pages, some for the first time, will depend on our ability to identify and locate them, determine their needs, and ensure that sufficient water is left in our rivers, streams, and aquifers to sustain them.

Thus, this third volume of River Books, a partnership between Texas A&M University Press and the River Systems Institute at Texas State University, is the most useful tool yet for fish identification. Even more important as we struggle for the continued existence of these fishes, *Freshwater Fishes of Texas* celebrates the great diversity of native fishes living in Texas inland waters. Unfortunately, that diversity has decreased in the last half century, and as many as five species of fish have become extinct in that time. Three more are extirpated from the state and fully twenty-five additional species are considered endangered, threatened, or of conservation concern. The primary cause of these losses has been inappropriate management of our water resources for uses other than the natural systems which depend on them.

Thanks to the intellect, skill, and dedication of Thomas, Bonner, and Whiteside, we now have an additional tool to ensure that the rivers and streams of our children and theirs will be as rich in aquatic life as they are today.

—Andrew Sansom

Foreword

I state the obvious in saying this book is for those who *want* to know how to identify Texas freshwater fishes. In field and laboratory courses I teach students how to identify Texas fishes and about their ecology and management, so naturally I am very glad (and I expect my students will be also) to have this field guide as a formal resource. But, who else would benefit from reading and using this guide?

As terrestrial creatures, we rarely look into (let alone enter) the watery world of fishes. Unlike birds, mammals, amphibians, reptiles, flowers, butterflies, and seashells, fish are less accessible to those who collect, photograph, and watch wildlife. Even so, a field guide to fishes is useful to those with a home aquarium or water garden, or who frequent museums and aquaria, and those with a snorkel and mask who travel to systems where fish can readily be seen through clear water. I also recommend this guide to those surrounded by muddy systems, like those near my own house. Once you see our Texas fishes and the maps of their distribution, you will want to read on and will be amazed to learn which fishes are probably living in your own nearby stream, pond, or creek (even though you might need a dip net or small seine to be able to view them up close). I hope that you will then wonder why certain fishes are found only here or there, whereas others seem to be everywhere. Perhaps you will further consider all the biological diversity in our water systems.

The photographs themselves are a significant contribution to the published literature on Texas fishes, and they are a very useful complement to the comprehensive and more technical scientific keys used to identify fish to the species level. Moreover, the photographs are combined with drawings and instructions that will help readers to locate various characteristics on a fish, to make certain measurements and counts that together distinguish families and species of fish, and to appreciate the importance and significance of the fish and its role in our water systems.

This book also provides the tools to do much more than spot the limited number of fishes that can be readily identified by a few easily seen characters (shape, color, markings, or a limited distribution in river drainages). Lest you take our aquatic biodiversity for granted, turn to the technical instructions in this guide. Here you can see how a biologist scientifically confirms a fish's identity. In addition to measuring and counting external features (scales, spines, and fin rays), it may also be necessary to use a microscope or dissection to further examine representatives of a group of similar looking fish for differences in other characteristics, such as length and coiling pattern of the intestine (giving insight into feeding preferences), color of the lining of the body cavity, number and shape of the teeth—not just on their jaws, but also their tongue, roof of their mouth, and bones encircling their throat. Just as birders refer to "LBB's" (little brown birds that seem at first to all look alike), their counterparts in the fish world are the many small-bodied species among the true minnows (those in the family Cyprinidae). So, do not despair that even with this guide (or even a technical key) you are still unsure of a fish's identity.

Whether you aspire to identify all the fishes in this guide or not, it will help you to realize that biologists entrusted to maintain the natural biodiversity and proper functioning of our water systems must sometimes look beyond scales and skin to verify a fish's identity. Even 'experts' can disagree as to the true identity of a fish, because of the range of natural variation—due to past and ongoing processes of change—contained in the biological diversity among individuals of even a single species. For example, you might be surprised at the range of color patterns exhibited by longear sunfish (*Lepomis megalotis*), or that even seasoned biologists can make honest mistakes when attempting to identify the common and ubiquitous red shiner (*Cyprinella lutrensis*), due to its variety of body shapes and colors during its life and across its distribution in so many types of habitat. Also, the young individuals of many fish species look more like each other than they do the adults of their own species, so even the experts will often seek a second opinion.

In the comments section of the species accounts, you will find interesting aspects of ecology and life history that might remind you of why it is so important to maintain the abundance, integrity, and variety of habitat types used by these fishes, and thereby preserve the functions in the ecological community and services to people that these systems provide. For example, biologists can determine the integrity and health of a water body based on samples of the species and families of fishes present, their abundance and tolerance of various water conditions (temperature, oxygen concentration, salinity, acidity, clarity), and their preferences for types or locations of foods. For instance, there are specialists—which feed on microscopic algae, or invertebrates in the water column, or insects that burrow into the stream bottom or attach to wood and rocks—and there are generalists who feed on any and all of these. Fishes that eat other fishes are important in monitoring for environmental contaminants, especially those like mercury that can enter our own food system.

As you read through the species accounts, you might begin to notice critical requirements common to several fish groups. These often are habitats or conditions needed for successful reproduction, such as sustained water flow during spring so that adults can swim into upstream segments to spawn so that their eggs and larvae have time to develop while being transported downstream. For some fish, appropriate rocks of the right size are needed for building nests, or aquatic vegetation must be present to which eggs can be attached and protected from suffocation by silt or washing away and in which young fish can hide from predators and yet still find food.

I hope many people read this guide and not only learn the names and locations of Texas fishes but also gather insight into responsible choices about the uses of our natural water bodies. These choices have consequences not just for the aquatic biota but for ourselves because they impact such important aspects of our lives, including recreation, food, waste disposal, irrigation, and even the mining of sand and gravel.

—Fran Gelwick

Acknowledgments

This field guide was developed to help both recreational anglers and serious students of ichthyology identify 161 species of Texas freshwater fishes. Biologists and resource managers will also find it useful as a supplement to the dichotomous key compiled by Hubbs et al. (1991) as well as a companion to other state field guides, such as *Fishes of Alabama* and *Fishes of Arkansas*.

The guide provides high resolution photographs, habitat information, physical descriptions, and range maps. The first sections of the book include a brief explanation of the species descriptions, a map of major drainage basins in the state, an explanation of certain counts and measurements, a discussion of the phylogeny of fishes, and a dichotomous key for the family classifications of freshwater fish in Texas. After the species accounts we include an appendix that describes how to count pharyngeal teeth. We also provide a glossary that includes both definitions and photographs of morphological structures.

In an effort to capture natural color patterns, Chad Thomas photographed most specimens within twenty-four to forty-eight hours of collection. Because colors differ between breeding and nonbreeding individuals and between males and females in some fishes, additional photographs were taken to display variability in color patterns. For some rare and endangered species, photographs were taken of preserved specimens held in the Texas State University Ichthyology Teaching Collection. Several threatened, endangered, and uncommon species known to occur in Texas are excluded from this guide because of collection restrictions (e.g., too few specimens exist, federal permit restrictions, etc.).

If it were not for the help of numerous individuals and their willingness to take time out of their busy schedules to help collect specimens or to assist with financial support, this guide would never have come together as it has. We are thankful to The Richan Fund and the River Systems Institute at Texas State University for funding to help cover publication costs. We would like to thank Dr. Francis Rose and the Biology Department at Texas State University for the initial funding that allowed us to advance this project from a rudimentary lab guide to a manuscript ready for publication. We thank Dr. Thomas Arsuffi for lending us the use of his digital camera and computer lab. We also owe many thanks to Dr. and Mrs. Glenn Longley; if it were not for their hospitality much more time would have been needed to complete this project. Special thanks go to Michelle Allison for her advice concerning photography and photo editing, which made many of the pictures in this book possible. We also thank Janet Wisian for her help in producing prints of the photographs to aid in the copy-editing process. We are especially grateful for the editorial comments of David Bass and an anonymous reviewer, which helped us refine the manuscript in order to produce a concise text.

We owe a debt of gratitude to those who helped with the collection of speci-mens for photographs: Casey Williams, Jackie Watson, Cheryl Hooker, Casey Hartl, Penny Pekar, Brad Littrell, Dusty McDonald, Bruce Kelley, Joe Martin, Nathan Pence, Chad Norris, John Burch, Preston Bean, Tracy Levy, Nadia Martinez, Gene Martinez, David Levine, David Bass, Bryan Cook, Dale Jurecka, Jason Woods, Ryan Kainer, Victor Castillo, Tom Heard, Daniel Pearson, Gilbert Trejo, Jennifer Neu, Trixi Deslisle, Mike Canova, Amanda Garcia, Milton Sun-vison, Evan Hornig, Dr. Chad Hargreaves, Dr. Tim Patton, Dr. Allen Rutherford, A. E. Wood State Fish Hatchery, and the students of Texas State University's fisheries management and ichthyology classes of 2002–2005.

About the Fish Descriptions

Habitat associations, life history information, physical characteristics, and other notes of interest are from published texts. A wealth of detailed ecological knowledge exists for many of the fishes described, but such information has been kept brief here to conform to the overall purpose and intent of this guide. For each species description the following sections are provided:

NAME: Common and scientific names follow the taxonomic nomenclature rules of the American Fisheries Society found in *Common and Scientific Names of Fishes from the United States, Canada, and Mexico,* sixth edition (2004). The author(s) of the original species description and the year are listed next. Parentheses around the author and year indicate that the fish was originally described under another name.

RANGE: The descriptions of species distribution list the major river drainages or areas where a species may be found and are based on reported occurrences in the referenced literature. The range maps display a more specific location within those drainages and areas where that particular fish may be found. The reader should keep in mind that there may be some inaccuracies as a result of localized extinctions and introductions.

HABITAT: Places where a species may be found are indicated by macrohabitat (e.g., rivers, creeks, natural lakes and reservoirs, swamps, ditches, and bayous) and microhabitat (e.g., channels, pools, riffles, runs, backwaters, and undercut banks).

CHARACTERISTICS: This list includes major external and some internal morphological features that may be used to help identify a particular species. The glossary provides definitions of these morphological features.

DIMENSIONS: Maximum standard length and weight are given in English (inches and pounds) and metric units (centimeters and kilograms). The data include expected upper limits of size but should not be taken as a reference for state or world record lengths and weights.

FIN COUNTS: Various fin ray counts may be used for identification. When available, an upper and lower range for each count is provided. Methodology for fin counts is provided in the section describing common counts and measurements of fishes.

COLORATION: Colors for living specimens in nonbreeding condition are given for body regions (dorsal, lateral, and ventral) and fins. For some fishes there is a description of breeding colors.

COMMENTS: Information in this category may include conservation status, unique or unusual life history traits, and characteristics that may distinguish particular species from similar looking species. Conservation status for fishes of Texas has been set by the Texas Parks and Wildlife Department (TP&WD) and defines fish as being either

(1) endangered—threatened with statewide extinction as determined by the executive director of TP&WD, or

(2) threatened—likely to become endangered in the future as determined by the TP&WD Commission.

Drainages of Texas

This map shows the state's major river drainages, which correspond to the species ranges included in the description of each fish. Large tributaries and smaller streams draining directly into the Gulf of Mexico are not included on this map.

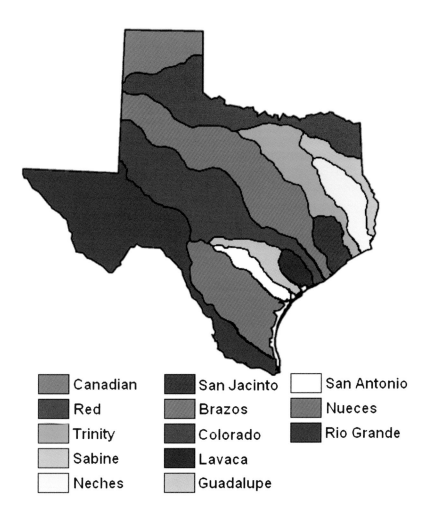

Canadian	San Jacinto	San Antonio
Red	Brazos	Nueces
Trinity	Colorado	Rio Grande
Sabine	Lavaca	
Neches	Guadalupe	

Common Counts and Measurements

This section describes and illustrates some of the methods of counting and measurement often used during fish identification. These methods are based on the work of Hubbs and Lagler (1949). Photographs of fish are helpful, but to be confident in identifying species one must make careful counts and measurements of fish anatomy as well as examining other distinguishing characteristics.

Counts

(1) Spine and fin ray count: dorsal, anal, and paired fins of class Actinopterygii might have hard fin spines, soft fin rays, or both. Soft rays are often branched and segmented, whereas spines are neither branched or segmented. For paired fins all rays are counted. When taking ray counts of dorsal and anal fins on minnows (Cyprinidae) and suckers (Catostomidae) usually the first two or three rays are short and splinterlike and are thus counted as one. The last ray, which will look separated all the way to its base and appear to be two rays, is also counted as just one ray. For the remainder of the families, all rays are counted.

(2) Lateral line count: following the lateral line, count from the first pored scale near the opercle to the last pored scale. For fishes with an incomplete lateral line or no lateral line, count the row of scales along the midlateral side.

(3) Cheek scale count: the number of scale rows crossed by a line from the eye orbit to the angle of the preopercle.

Measurements

(1) Total length: distance from the farthest tip (i.e., snout or jaw) to the end of the longest ray when the caudal fin is compressed.

(2) Body depth: greatest body depth not including fleshy or scaly portions of fin bases.

(3) Predorsal length: distance from dorsal fin origin to tip of snout.

(4) Fin base length: distance from fin origin (anterior) of fin to insertion (posterior).

(5) Head length: distance from tip of snout to posterior end of the opercular membrane, including any fleshy extension of the opercle membrane, such as that on the redbreast sunfish.

(6) Snout length: distance from the tip of the snout to anterior bony orbital rim.

Phylogeny of Fishes

This section presents an overview of fish evolution to help the reader understand relationships among the chordate animals generally known as fish. Phylogeny describes the evolutionary history and relationships of taxonomic groups. The term "fish" represents not one but several extinct and extant monophyletic groups of organisms that first arose and began radiating some 570 million years ago (Kent and Carr 2001). Current classification schemes have living fishes assigned to two superclasses (Agnatha, or jawless chordates, and Gnathostomata, or jawed chordates) and to five classes (Bond 1996). Two fishes found in Texas, the southern brook lamprey and chestnut lamprey, belong in superclass Agnatha, class Cephlaspidomorpha. All other freshwater fishes of Texas described in this guide belong to class Actinopterygii, formerly referred to as class Osteichthyes.

Within class Actinopterygii, sturgeons and paddlefishes (family Acipenseridae and Polyodontidae, respectively) are living descendants of a lineage that appeared some 400 million years ago (Kent and Carr 2001). Ancestors of the remaining members of Actinopterygii appeared some 250 million years ago. Early ancestors of gars (family Lepisosteidae) and bowfins (family Amiidae) appeared first, followed by ancestors of goldeyes (family Hiodontidae, found only in the Red River), freshwater eels (family Anguillidae), and shads (family Clupeidae). During this radiation period, one supercontinent called Pangaea comprised the earth's entire land mass. Around 180 million years ago, the one land mass split into two continents (Laurasia and Gondwanaland) about the time ancestors of the Otophysi group and the ancestors of pickerels (family Escocidae), trouts (family Salmonidae), and pirate perches (family Aphredoderidae) appeared (Moyle and Cech 2000). Some 65 million years ago the Otophysi ancestors gave rise to early ancestors of bullhead catfishes (family Ictaluridae), minnows (family Cyprinidae), suckers (family Catostomidae), and tetras (family Characidae). Also some 65 million years ago, early ancestors arose for the remaining families of Texas freshwater fishes, such as mullets (family Mugilidae), silversides (family Atherinidae), livebearers (family Poeciliidae), killifishes (family Fundulidae), pupfishes (family Cyprinodontidae),

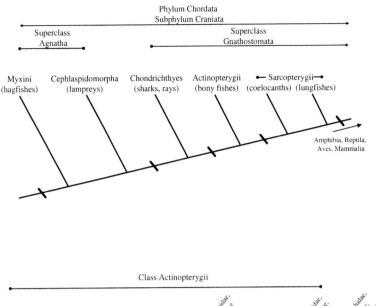

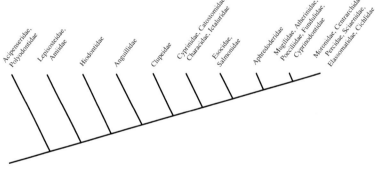

temperate basses (family Moronidae), sunfishes (family Centrarchidae), darters (family Percidae), drums (family Sciaenidae), pygmy sunfishes (family Elassomatidae), and cichlids (family Cichlidae). During the past 65 million years North America separated from Asia, allowing several ancestors of these families to radiate only on one continent. Consequently, several families of fish (e.g., Ictaluridae, Centrarchidae) occur naturally only within waters of North America (Moyle and Cech 2000). Thereafter, North American glaciation events and habitat diversity shaped and formed the radiation of these groups into numerous lineages, eventually giving rise to the species we have today.

Key to the Families

This section is written in dichotomous format, which is a series of "yes" or "no" paired questions based on morphological characters that should identify each fish to only one family. The final step in the key leads you to the page where descriptions of species of that family begin. Morphological differences among families are relatively large and easy to recognize; thus the key can be used as quick reference to identify a fish, but it also highlights similarities and differences between the fish families. Unfamiliar terms encountered in the key may be found in the glossary.

1a. Jawless, mouth disc shaped; 7 pairs of external gill openings; paired fins absent; single nostril positioned medially . . . . .Lampreys—Petromyzontidae (pp. 15–16)
1b. Mouth with jaws; paired fins present (pectoral or pelvic or both); 1 gill opening on each side of the head; 1 or 2 nostril openings on each side of the head 2

2a. Body snakelike; lacks pelvic fins; dorsal, anal, and caudal fins joined . . . . .American eel—Anguillidae (p. 25)
2b. Body more fishlike; caudal fin either heterocercal (backbone extending well into the upper lobe of caudal fin), abbreviated heterocercal (backbone only extending slightly into upper lobe of caudal fin, or homocercal (backbone does not extend into upper lobe of caudal fin and forms a hypural plate) 3

3a. Caudal fin either heterocercal or abbreviated heterocercal. 4
3b. Caudal fin homocercal. 7

4a. Caudal fin heterocercal, body with bony scutes (plates)or appears scaleless. . 5
4b. Caudal fin abbreviated heterocercal; body covered with ganoid or cycloid scales 6

5a. Long, paddle-shaped snout; scaleless except for a few ganoid scales at the base of caudal fin . . . . .Paddlefish—Polyodontidae (p. 18)
5b. Snout conical or shovel-shaped with four barbels on ventral surface; several rows of bony scutes (plates) along body . . . . .Sturgeons—Acipenseridae (p. 17)

6a. Body covered with ganoid scales; snout formed into a beak; gular plate absent . . . . .Gars—Lepisosteidae (pp. 19–22)
6b. Body covered with cycloid scales; snout not formed into a beak; gular plate present . . . . .Bowfin—Amiidae (p. 23)

7a. One dorsal fin; pelvic fins without spines. 8
7b. One or two dorsal fins; pelvic fins with spines. 16

8a. Adipose fin present. 9
8b. Adipose fin not present. 12

9a. Scales on body present; barbels on head absent. .10
9b. Scales on body absent; barbels on head present; if barbels absent, body with bony plates 11

10a. Fewer than 50 lateral line scales; incisor teeth present . . . . Tetras—Characidae (p. 92)
10b. More than 60 lateral line scales; incisor teeth absent . . . . Trouts—Salmonidae (p. 106)

11a. Barbels absent, body covered with bony plates. . . . . .Suckermouth catfishes—Loricariidae (p. 103)
11b. Scales absent; head with 4–8 barbels . . . . Bullhead catfishes—Ictaluridae (pp. 93–102)

12a. Head lacks scales 13
12b. Head partially scaled 16

13a. Anal fin with 17 or more rays 14
13b. Anal fin with fewer than 13 rays 15

14a. Belly with scales forming a sawlike keel . . . . Shads—
    Clupeidae (pp. 26–27)

14b. Belly without scales forming a sawlike keel . . . . .Goldeye—
    Hiodontidae (p. 24)

15a. Inferior, fleshy mouth modified for sucking; more than 7 pharyngeal teeth
    in main row; usually 10 or more dorsal fin rays . . . . Suckers—
    Catostomidae (pp. 83–91)

15b. Mouth usually not fleshy or modified for sucking; fewer than 7 pharyngeal
    teeth in main row; usually 10 or fewer dorsal fin rays (excluding common
    carp and goldfish) . . . . .Carps and minnows—Cyprinidae (pp. 28–82)

16a. Jaws duckbilled; caudal fin forked; lateral line present . . . . Pickerels—
    Esocidae (pp. 104-105)

16b. Jaws not duckbilled; caudal fin rounded; lateral line absent. 17

17a. Pelvic anal fins with 1–7 spines; 1–2 dorsal fins 20

17b. Caudal fin rounded; lateral line absent 18

18a. Mature males with rounded anal fin; males and females with third anal fin
    ray branched; no gonopodium present 19

18b. Mature males with pointed anal fin forming a gonopodium; males and
    females with third anal fin ray unbranched. . . . . .Livebearers—
    Poeciliidae (pp. 113-118)

19a. Body robust; teeth in single row are incisorlike and tricuspid (three points
    on a tooth) . . . . .Pupfishes—Cyprinodontidae (pp. 127–29)

19b. Body elongate; conical (cone-shaped) pointed teeth in a single row or
    several rows . . . . .Killifishes—Fundulidae (pp. 119–26)

20a. Anus anterior to pelvic fins (adults); more than 5 soft rays on each pelvic
    fin . . . . .Pirate perch—Aphredoderidae (p. 107)

20b. Anus posterior to pelvic fins; 5 soft rays on pelvic fins. 21

21a. Pelvic fin position abdominal or subthoracic; dorsal fins widely
    separated 22

21b. Pelvic fin position thoracic; dorsal fins joined or, if separate, closely adjacent to one another 23

22a. Dorsal fin with 4 thick spines; anal fin with 2–3 spines; adipose eyelids present . . . . .Mullets—Mugilidae (pp. 108–109)

22b. Dorsal fin with 4–8 thin spines; anal fin with 1 spine; adipose eyelids absent . . . . .Silversides—Atherinidae (pp. 110–12)

23a. One nare (nostril) on each side of head; lateral line incomplete . . . . .Cichlids—Cichlidae (pp. 174–75)

23b. Two nares (nostrils) on each side of head; lateral line complete, incomplete, or absent nostrils 24

24a. Dorsal fin with more than 23 fin rays; lateral line extends to tip of caudal fin . . . . .Drums—Sciaenidae (p. 172)

24b. Dorsal fin with fewer than 23 fin rays; lateral line, if present, does not extend to tip of caudal fin 25

25a. Anal fin with 1–2 spines . . . . .Walleye and darters—Percidae (pp. 151-171)

25b. Anal fin with 3–8 spines. 26

26a. Posterior margin of operculum with a sharp spine; spiny and soft dorsal fin separate or only slightly connected; pseudobranchium present and exposed . . . . .Temperate basses—Moronidae (pp. 130–33)

26b. Posterior margin of operculum without a sharp spine; spiny and soft dorsal fins connected or with deep notch; pseudobranchium covered or absent 27

27a. Lateral line present or incomplete; adults longer than 1.5 in (38.1 mm) . . . . .Black basses and sunfishes—Centrarchidae (pp. 134–50)

27b. Lateral line absent; adults longer than 1.5 in (38.1mm) . . . . Pygmy sunfish—Elassomatidae (p. 173)

Species Accounts

Chestnut lamprey, *Ichthyomyzon castaneus,* view of sucking disc

Chestnut lamprey, *Ichthyomyzon castaneus,* 6.2 in (157 mm)

Chestnut Lamprey

Ichthyomyzon castaneus Girard, 1858

RANGE: Red, Sabine, and Neches river basins.

HABITAT: Lakes and creeks. Parasitic adults are found in open water areas often attached to other fish.

CHARACTERISTICS:

(1) Sucking disc wider than head; disc length contained 14.3 times in total length.

(2) Teeth of sucking disc sharp and well developed.

(3) Single median nostril.

(4) Seven gill openings.

(5) Myomeres (muscle segments): 47–58.

(6) Intestine well developed.

DIMENSIONS: Up to 15 in (381 mm).

COLORATION: Dorsal and lateral regions yellow or brown; ventral region olive-yellow to white. After spawning, adults take on a blue-black coloration.

COMMENTS: During spawning, adults migrate to headwater streams and use their sucking disc to carry stones to excavate and maintain nest pits. See southern brook lamprey, *Ichthyomyzon gagei.*

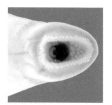

Southern brook lamprey, *Ichthyomyzon gagei*, view of sucking disc

Southern brook lamprey, *Ichthyomyzon gagei*, adult, 6 in (152 mm)

Southern brook lamprey, *Ichthyomyzon gagei*, ammocoete, 2.5 in (63.5 mm)

Southern Brook Lamprey

Ichthyomyzon gagei Hubbs and Trautman, 1937

RANGE: Red, Trinity, San Jacinto, Sabine, and Neches river basins.
HABITAT: Rivers and creeks.
CHARACTERISTICS:

(1) Sucking disc small; disc length contained 17.2 to 26.3 times in total length.
(2) Teeth in posterior field (or entire field) of sucking disc poorly developed.
(3) Single median nostril.
(4) Gill openings: 7.
(5) Myomeres (muscle segments): 40–59.

(6) Intestine poorly developed.
DIMENSIONS: Up to 7 in (178 mm).
COLORATION: Dorsal and lateral regions gray or olive; ventral region yellow.
COMMENTS: Adults use the sucking disc to carry stones to build and maintain nest pits. Nonparasitic adults move upstream to spawn and then die. Ammocoetes (larval form) burrow into the substrate of rivers and creeks where they filter feed for a year or more before maturing into adults. The southern brook lamprey can be distinguished from the chestnut lamprey by the small mouth disc and small adult size. The two species might also be distinguished from one another in that the adult southern brook lamprey is a nonparasitic form with a poorly developed intestine whereas the adult chestnut lamprey is parasitic with a well-developed intestine.

Shovelnose sturgeon, *Scaphirhynchus platorynchus,* 12 in (305 mm)

Shovelnose Sturgeon

Scaphirhynchus platorynchus

(Rafinesque, 1820)

RANGE: Red River below Lake Texoma's Denison Dam.

HABITAT: Rivers. Habitat and range have been reduced by the construction of dams.

CHARACTERISTICS:

(1) Snout shovel shaped.

(2) Barbels (4) on the ventral surface of snout.

(3) Mouth inferior.

(4) Inner barbels more than half the length of outer barbels.

(5) Lower lip with 4 lobes.

(6) Upper lobe of caudal fin with long filament; some specimens might have filament broken off.

(7) Longitudinal rows of bony plates on dorsal and lateral region.

(8) Caudal fin heterocercal.

DIMENSIONS: Up to 3 ft (914 mm) and 10 lbs (4.5 kg).

FIN COUNTS: Anal soft fin rays 18–23; dorsal soft fin rays 30–36.

COLORATION: Dorsal and lateral regions brown or gray; ventral region white.

COMMENTS: The shovelnose sturgeon was once considered a "trash" fish by anglers, but properly prepared the flesh of shovelnose sturgeon is considered a delicacy and its eggs are highly sought after for caviar. This species is listed by the state as threatened.

Paddlefish,
*Polyodon
spathula,* 8 in
(203 mm)

Paddlefish

Polyodon spathula (Walbaum, 1972)

RANGE: The paddlefish was once found in drainages from the Trinity River eastward to the Sabine River.

HABITAT: Rivers. The paddlefish might also be found in lakes and reservoirs as result of restoration projects. Habitat and range have been reduced due to the damming of rivers and other habitat alterations.

CHARACTERISTICS:
(1) Long, paddle-shaped snout.
(2) Large jaws with small teeth.
(3) Posterior margin of opercle terminates as a long pointed flap.
(4) Small ganoid scales on the base of the upper lobe of caudal fin.
(5) Caudal fin heterocercal.

DIMENSIONS: Up to 7.3 ft (2.2 m) and 150 lbs (68 kg).

FIN COUNTS: Anal soft fin rays 50–65; dorsal soft fin rays 50–60.

COLORATION: Dorsal and lateral regions gray to dark blue-gray; ventral region silvery white. Operculum with black and blue spots.

COMMENTS: The paddlefish is a filter feeder. The purpose of the paddle-shaped snout may be for stabilization while swimming with the mouth open as feeding occurs or for detecting concentrations of plankton (the paddle is covered with taste buds). Like the eggs of the sturgeon, the eggs of paddlefish are sought after as caviar, and the meat is considered excellent eating. This species is listed by the state as threatened.

Alligator gar, *Atractosteus spatula,* 2 ft (610 mm)

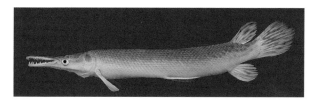

Alligator Gar

Atractosteus spatula (Lacépède, 1803)

RANGE: Rivers and creeks from the Red River to the Rio Grande.

HABITAT: Usually found in lakes, swamps, and bayous, as well as pools and backwaters of rivers. The alligator gar is very tolerant of brackish and marine environments.

CHARACTERISTICS:

(1) Large canine teeth in two rows on each side of the upper jaw; one row on lower jaw. The young of other gar species possess two rows of teeth on each side of the upper jaw but only retain one row as they mature.

(2) Snout short and blunt, narrowest width contained 4.5 or fewer times in snout length; distance from tip of snout to the corner of the mouth slightly shorter than the distance from the corner of the mouth to posterior edge of opercle.

(3) Lateral line scales: 58–62.

(4) Spots on median fins and posterior portion of body; may not be notable on some specimens.

(5) Abbreviated heterocercal caudal fin.

DIMENSIONS: Can reach up to 10 ft (3 m) and 302 lbs (137 kg).

COLORATION: Dorsal and lateral regions dark olive-brown to black; ventral region yellow to white. Fins are dark brown, and spots may be notable on median fins; some specimens may have spots on the body.

COMMENTS: The adult alligator gar may be distinguished from other gars by its short, broad snout and two rows of canine teeth in the upper jaw. For all gar species, the air bladder is connected to the pharynx and can be used as a breathing organ, allowing these fish to "gulp air" when the oxygen level in the water is low.

Spotted gar,
*Lepisosteus
oculatus,* 1.9 ft
(584 mm)

Spotted Gar

Lepisosteus oculatus Winchell, 1864

RANGE: Red River south to the Rio Grande basin.

HABITAT: Creeks in pools and backwaters, rivers in oxbow lakes, swamps, and drainage ditches.

CHARACTERISTICS:

(1) Large canine teeth in one row on each side of the upper and lower jaws.

(2) Snout of medium length and width; width at nostrils 1.0–1.5 times the eye diameter. Length from tip of snout to corner of mouth greater than length from corner of mouth to the back edge of operculum.

(3) Lateral line scales: 54–59.

(4) Caudal fin abbreviated hetero-cercal.

(5) Spots on body, head, and all fins; those taken from turbid water might lack spots on top of head and snout, but spots will still be on the sides of the head and snout.

DIMENSIONS: Up to 3.8 ft (1.2 m) and 15 lbs (6.8 kg).

FIN COUNTS: Anal soft fin rays 8–9; dorsal soft fin rays 6–9; pectoral soft fin rays 10–11; pelvic soft fin rays 6.

COLORATION: Spots on body, head, and all fins. Dorsal region black or dark green; lateral region olive-brown; ventral region white to pale yellow. Juveniles have a broad, brown middorsal stripe that might break up into a row of spots posteriorly; they also have a dark brown midlateral stripe with a thin, brown stripe above it forming into spots posteriorly. The ventral region of juveniles is dark brown.

COMMENTS: An adult spotted gar may be distinguished from other gar species by dark spots on the dorsal region of the head.

Longnose gar,
Lepisosteus osseus,
2 ft (610 mm)

Longnose Gar

Lepisosteus osseus (Linnaeus, 1758)

RANGE: Statewide.

HABITAT: Lakes and rivers with backwaters, oxbow lakes, and pools.

CHARACTERISTICS:

(1) Large canine teeth in single row on each side of the upper and lower jaws.

(2) Snout long and narrow; narrowest width contained in snout length 10 or more times. Snout width at nostrils less than eye diameter.

(3) Spots on median fins; those taken from clear water often have spots on body, while those taken from turbid water will usually lack body spots.

(4) Lateral line scales: 57–63.

(5) Caudal fin abbreviated heterocercal.

DIMENSIONS: Up to 6.4 ft (1.95 m) and 82 lbs (37.2 kg).

FIN COUNTS: Anal soft fin rays 8–10; dorsal soft fin rays 6–9; pectoral soft fin rays 10–13; pelvic soft fin rays 6.

COLORATION: Dorsal and lateral region olive-brown; ventral region white. Median fins have dark brown spots and all fins might be tinted orange. Juveniles have a thin, dark middorsal stripe and a broad, black midlateral stripe; the dorsal margin of the midlateral band is scalloped or merges with a row of red-brown spots. Some specimens may have dark spots on the top of the snout.

COMMENTS: An adult longnose gar may be distinguished from other gar species by its long, thin snout. For all gar species, the air bladder is connected to the pharynx and can be used as a breathing organ, allowing these fish to "gulp air" when the oxygen level in the water is low.

Shortnose gar, *Lepisosteus platostomus,* 2.23 ft (686 mm)

Shortnose Gar

Lepisosteus platostomus Rafinesque, 1820

RANGE: Red River basin below Lake Texoma.

HABITAT: Usually found in lakes, swamps, rivers, and creeks with pools and backwaters.

CHARACTERISTICS:

(1) Large canine teeth in one row on each side of the upper and lower jaws.

(2) Snout of medium length and width; width at nostrils 1.0–1.5 times the eye diameter. Length from tip of snout to corner of mouth greater than length from corner of mouth to the back edge of operculum.

(3) Lateral line scales: 59–64.

(4) Caudal fin abbreviated heterocercal.

DIMENSIONS: May reach 19 lbs (8.6 kg).

COLORATION: Dorsal and lateral regions olive-green with a few dark spots on the body and fins, although spots may not be seen on some specimens; ventral region white.

COMMENTS: The shortnose gar may be distinguished from other species of gar by its short snout, lack of spots on the top of the head, and single row of large canine teeth on the upper jaw. For all gar species, the air bladder is connected to the pharynx and can be used as a breathing organ, allowing these fish to "gulp air" when the oxygen level in the water is low.

Bowfin, *Amia calva,*
11 in (279 mm)

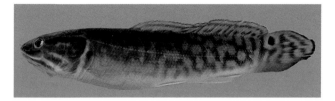

Bowfin

Amia calva Linnaeus, 1766

RANGE: Red, San Jacinto, Sabine river basins and lower reaches of the Colorado and Brazos river basins.

HABITAT: Rivers and creeks with backwaters; swamps, sloughs, ponds, and lakes.

CHARACTERISTICS:

(1) Three stripes on sides of head; may be faded or absent on adults.

(2) Large mouth; upper jaw extends beyond eye.

(3) Gular plate on chin large and bony.

(4) Tubular nostrils.

(5) Long dorsal fin, more than half the length of the dorsal region.

(6) Lateral line scales: 65–70.

(7) Black spot with a thin border of yellow or orange on the upper portion of caudal fin base, which might be faded or absent on non-breeding males and female adults.

(8) Caudal fin abbreviated hetero-cercal.

DIMENSIONS: Up to 3 ft (914 mm) and 20 lbs (9.1 kg).

FIN COUNTS: Anal soft fin rays 11–12; dorsal soft fin rays 42–53; pectoral soft fin rays 17–18; pelvic soft fin rays 7; caudal soft fin rays 25–28.

COLORATION: Dorsal and lateral regions mottled olive; ventral region yellow to pale green; ventral fins turquoise-green with black margins; dorsal and caudal fin dark green with black stripes. Breeding males have lips, throat, belly, and ventral fins that are turquoise-green.

COMMENTS: Similar to the gar, the bowfin's air bladder is connected to the pharynx and can be used as a breathing organ.

Goldeye, *Hiodon alosoides,* 12 in (305 mm)

Goldeye

Hiodon alosoides (Rafinesque, 1819)

RANGE: Red River basin; it is abundant in Lake Texoma.

HABITAT: Usually found in lakes, reservoirs, and rivers with deep pools and channels.

CHARACTERISTICS:

(1) Eyes with adipose eyelids.

(2) Canine teeth on jaws and tongue.

(3) Mouth large with maxillary extending beyond pupil of eye.

(4) Lateral line scales: 57–62.

(5) Ventral keel from pectoral fin base to anal fin; keel does not have a sawtoothed margin.

DIMENSIONS: May reach 1.7 ft (50.8 cm) and 3.2 lbs (1.4 kg).

FIN COUNTS: Anal soft fin rays 30–32; dorsal soft fin rays 9–10; pectoral soft fin rays 11–12; pelvic soft fin rays 7.

COLORATION: Dorsal region pale green; lateral region silvery white to slightly brassy; ventral region white.

COMMENTS: The goldeye is a nocturnal species; its eyes are adapted for low light and turbid conditions, having only rods (detect light) and no cones (detect color).

American eel,
Anguilla rostrata,
11.5 in (292 mm)

American Eel

Anguilla rostrata (Lesueur, 1817)

RANGE: Red River to the Rio Grande; no longer found in far western portions of Texas.

HABITAT: Rivers and creeks. During the day, eels hide in undercut banks and deep pools with logs and boulders. Habitat and range have been reduced by the construction of dams.

CHARACTERISTICS:

(1) Slightly compressed, snakelike body.
(2) Jaws with well-developed teeth.
(3) One gill slit in front of each pectoral fin.
(4) Long dorsal fin that is continuous with caudal and anal fins.
(5) Pelvic fins absent.
(6) Scales small and embedded.

DIMENSIONS: Up to 4.3 ft (1.3 m) and 7.5 lbs (3.4 kg).

COLORATION: Dorsal and lateral region olive to olive brown; ventral region pale yellow to white. Breeding specimens take on a gray coloration.

COMMENTS: The American eel is a catadromous species; adults migrate to the Sargasso Sea (in the western Atlantic Ocean) to spawn. Ribbon-shaped (leptocephalus) larvae are planktonic and are carried by currents to the coast of North America. Larvae metamorphose into "glass eels" and move upstream into rivers to mature into adults.

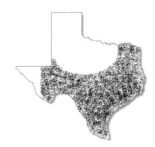

Gizzard shad, *Dorosoma cepedianum,* 9 in (229 mm)

Gizzard Shad

Dorosoma cepedianum (Lesueur, 1818)

RANGE: Statewide.
HABITAT: Open water areas of lakes, reservoirs, and rivers.
CHARACTERISTICS:
(1) Snout blunt.
(2) Mouth subterminal; premaxillary notch present.
(3) Black shoulder spot equal to or larger than eye pupil; spot may be faded or absent on adults.
(4) Last ray of dorsal fin greatly elongated; may be absent on juveniles or broken off on adults.
(5) Dorsal region with 6–8 dark, horizontal stripes.
(6) Belly scales form sharp-edged scutes resembling a sawtooth margin; 17–19 scutes in front of pelvic fin.
(7) Lateral line absent; 52–70 lateral series scales.
DIMENSIONS: Up to 20.5 in (521 mm) and 3.5 lbs (1.6 kg).
FIN COUNTS: Anal soft fin rays 29–33; dorsal soft fin rays 10–13; pectoral soft fin rays 15; pelvic soft fin rays 8.
COLORATION: Dorsal region blue-green with 6–8 dark, horizontal stripes; lateral region silver-white with black shoulder spot; ventral region silver-white.
COMMENTS: Gizzard shad may be thought of as good forage for game fish, but a rapid growth rate (4–7 inches in the first year) can make this fish too large to be eaten by all but the largest predators.

Threadfin shad,
*Dorosoma pete-
nense,* 3.5 in
(89 mm)

Threadfin Shad

Dorosoma petenense (Gunther, 1867)

RANGE: Throughout most of the eastern portions of the state; widely introduced into reservoirs as a forage fish.

HABITAT: Open water areas of lakes, reservoirs, and rivers.

CHARACTERISTICS:

(1) Mouth terminal.

(2) Black specks on chin and floor of mouth.

(3) Black shoulder spot smaller than pupil; might be absent on adults.

(4) Last ray of dorsal fin greatly elongated; might be absent on juveniles.

(5) Belly scales form sharp-edged scutes resembling a sawtooth margin; fewer than 17 scutes in front of pelvic fin.

(6) Lateral line absent; 40–48 lateral series scales.

DIMENSIONS: Up to 9 in (229 mm).

FIN COUNTS: Anal soft fin rays 24–28; dorsal soft fin rays 11–14.

COLORATION: Dorsal region blue-green with yellow hue; lateral region silver-white with black shoulder spot; ventral region silver-white. Fins are yellow except for dorsal fin.

COMMENTS: A threadfin shad can be distinguished from a gizzard shad by its pointed snout, terminal mouth, fewer scutes in front of pelvic fins, yellow fins, smaller adult size, and black chin specks on chin and floor of mouth. This species is very sensitive to temperature fluctuations; temperatures below 50° F can result in kills.

Central stoneroller, *Campostoma anomalum,* breeding adult, 4 in (102 mm)

Central stoneroller, *Campostoma anomalum,* nonbreeding adult, 3.5 in (89 mm)

Central Stoneroller

Campostoma anomalum (Rafinesque, 1820)

RANGE: River basins of the Edwards Plateau region as well as portions of the Brazos, San Jacinto, Red, and Trinity Rivers. This species can also be found as far as west as the Devils and Pecos Rivers.

HABITAT: Headwaters, rivers, and creeks in riffles, runs, and pools.

CHARACTERISTICS:

(1) Snout blunt and rounded.

(2) Mouth subterminal.

(3) Pharyngeal teeth 0,4-4,0; also 1,4-4,0 or 1,4-4,1.

(4) Cartilaginous ridge of lower jaw prominent and separated by a groove from the lower lip.

(5) Black midlateral stripe from tip of snout ending just before or in a small, round caudal spot; may be absent on adults.

(6) Lateral region with speckled pattern caused by replacement scales.

(7) Lateral line scales: 41–58.

(8) Long, coiled intestine wound around swim bladder.

DIMENSIONS: Up to 8.5 in (216 mm).

FIN COUNTS: Anal soft fin rays 7; dorsal soft fin rays 8; pectoral soft fin rays 15; pelvic soft fin rays 8.

COLORATION: Dorsal region olive-gray; lateral region olive-gray fading at midline with speckled pattern caused by replacement scales; ventral region white. Fins of nonbreeding stonerollers are colorless; breeding males have fins (excluding pectorals) with orange, black, and yellow bands. Juveniles have a black midlateral stripe and caudal spot.

COMMENTS: See Mexican stoneroller (*Campostoma ornatum*).

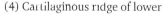

Mexican stoneroller, *Campostoma ornatum*, 3.2 in (81 mm)

Mexican Stoneroller

Campostoma ornatum Girard, 1856

RANGE: Rio Grande drainage.
HABITAT: Headwaters and creeks in pools and riffles.
CHARACTERISTICS:
(1) Snout blunt and rounded.
(2) Mouth subterminal; lower jaw length greater than eye length.
(3) Pharyngeal teeth 0,4-4,0; also 1,4-4,0 or 1,4-4,1.
(4) Cartilaginous ridge of lower jaw prominent and separated by a definite groove from the lower lip.
(5) Lateral region with speckled pattern caused by replacement scales.
(6) Lateral line scales: 58–77.
(7) Long, coiled intestine partially wound around swim bladder.
DIMENSIONS: Up to 6.3 in (160 mm).
FIN COUNTS: Anal soft fin rays 7; dorsal soft fin rays 8; pectoral soft fin rays 15; pelvic soft fin rays 8.

COLORATION: Dorsal region olive-gray; lateral region olive-gray fading at midline with speckled pattern caused by replacement scales; ventral region white. Juveniles have a black midlateral stripe and caudal spot.
COMMENTS: The Mexican stoneroller may be distinguished from the central stoneroller (*Campostoma anomalum*) by its higher lateral line scale count, larger mouth, and intestine that is only partially wound around the swim bladder. The cartilaginous ridge of the lower jaw is used to scrape algae, diatoms, and other food items off of rocks. This species is listed by the state as threatened.

Goldfish, *Carassius auratus*,
3.6 in (91 mm)

Goldfish

Carassius auratus (Linnaeus, 1758)

RANGE: Statewide; an exotic introduced from Asia and found as a result of bait bucket and aquarium releases.

HABITAT: Ponds, lakes, and rivers in pools and backwaters.

CHARACTERISTICS:

(1) Mouth terminal.

(2) Pharyngeal teeth 0,4-4,0.

(3) Elongate dorsal fin with more than 15 soft rays.

(4) Dorsal and anal fin with single hardened, serrated ray with 2 smaller hardened rays anterior to serrated ray.

(5) Lateral line scales: 26–29.

DIMENSIONS: Up to 16 in (406 mm).

FIN COUNTS: Anal soft fin rays 5–6; dorsal soft fin rays 15–21; pectoral soft fin rays 15–17; pelvic soft fin rays 8–9.

COLORATION: "Wild" goldfish have dorsal and upper lateral region that is olive-brown with bronze sheen; lower lateral and ventral region a light shade of brown with fins olive or colorless. Goldfish released from aquaria or bait buckets have blotches of black, red, and orange.

COMMENTS: Goldfish differ from common carp only in that they lack barbels; the two species can hybridize.

Grass carp, *Cteno-
pharyngodon idella,*
14.5 in (368 mm)

Grass Carp

Ctenopharyngodon idella (Valenciennes, 1844)

RANGE: Statewide; exotic introduced from Asia as biocontrol for
aquatic vegetation.

HABITAT: Rivers in pools and backwaters, as well as lakes and ponds.

CHARACTERISTICS:

(1) Mouth terminal.

(2) Pharyngeal teeth 2,4-4,2 or
2,5-4,2; teeth in main row with
grooves.

(3) Dorsal and lateral scales diamond
shaped and outlined by dark pigment.

(4) Lateral line scales: 37–42.

(5) Anal fin close to caudal fin; distance from front of anal fin base to
caudal fin base extends more than
2.5 times into distance from front
of anal fin base to tip of snout.

DIMENSIONS: Usually 20 lbs
(9.1 kg); up to 4 ft (1.2 m) and
100 lbs (45.4 kg).

FIN COUNTS: Anal soft fin rays
8–10; dorsal soft fin rays 8; pectoral
soft fin rays 15–17; pelvic soft fin rays
8–9.

COLORATION: Dorsal and lateral
region olive to silvery with scales outlined by dark pigment; ventral region
white.

COMMENTS: Adult grass carp con-
sume large quantities of aquatic vegetation and have been used to control
noxious aquatic plants, most notably
hydrilla (*Hydrilla verticillata*). However, due to the ability of this species
to eliminate vegetation, consider-
ations must be given to stocking den-
sity, desired vegetation coverage, and
escapement.

Plateau shiner, *Cyprinella lepida,* breeding adult, 2.2 in (56 mm)

Plateau shiner, *Cyprinella lepida,* nonbreeding adult, 2 in (51 mm)

Plateau Shiner

Cyprinella lepida Girard, 1856

RANGE: Nueces River basin.
HABITAT: Rivers and creeks with spring outflows.
CHARACTERISTICS:
(1) Head blunt and rounded.
(2) Pharyngeal teeth 1,4–4,1 or 2,4–4,2.
(3) Mouth subterminal.

(4) Black stripe on chin, extending no farther posteriorly than below eye. Chin stripe absent or faded on some individuals.
(5) Body slender.
(6) Purple triangle-shaped bar above pectoral fins; most notable on breeding males.
(7) Dorsal fin with dark pigment distributed equally throughout fin membrane; may be absent.
DIMENSIONS: Up to 3 in (76 mm).
COLORATION: Dorsal region olive; lateral region silvery; ventral region white. Dorsal region of breeding males green; lateral region yellow-purple with purple triangle-shaped bar above pectoral fin base. Head is gold-orange, and fins are yellow-orange.

Red shiner, *Cyprinella lutrensis,* breeding adult, 2.5 in (64 mm)

Red shiner, *Cyprinella lutrensis,* nonbreeding adult, 2.2 in (56 mm)

Red Shiner

Cyprinella lutrensis (Baird and Girard, 1853)

RANGE: Statewide.

HABITAT: Rivers and creeks in pools, runs, and riffles.

CHARACTERISTICS:

(1) Mouth nearly terminal.

(2) Pharyngeal teeth 0,4-4,0 also 1,4-4,1 or 0,4-4,1.

(3) Head sharp and compressed.

(4) Black stripe on chin, extending no farther posteriorly than below eye. Chin stripe absent or faded on some individuals.

(5) Dorsal and lateral scale edges outlined by dark pigment.

(6) Purple triangle-shaped bar above pectoral fins; most notable on breeding males.

(7) Dorsal fin with dark pigment distributed equally throughout fin membrane; may be absent.

(8) Lateral line scales: 32–36.

DIMENSIONS: Up to 3 in (76 mm).

FIN COUNTS: Anal soft fin rays 8; dorsal soft fin rays 8–10; pectoral soft fin rays 13–15.

COLORATION: Dorsal region olive; lateral region silvery with dark pigment on caudal peduncle forming a faint midlateral stripe; ventral region white. Fins are a light shade of red. Breeding males have blue dorsal and lateral regions; triangle-shaped bar above pectoral fins purple. Fins of breeding males are bright red.

COMMENTS: Red shiners are a popular aquarium species and are sold in pet stores under the name rainbow dace.

Proserpine shiner, *Cyprinella proserpina*, breeding adult, 2.5 in (64 mm)

Proserpine shiner, *Cyprinella proserpina*, nonbreeding adult, 2.2 in (56 mm)

Proserpine Shiner

Cyprinella proserpina (Girard, 1856)

RANGE: Rio Grande drainage: the Devils and lower Pecos Rivers as well as Las Moras, Pintos, and San Felipe Creeks.

HABITAT: Rivers and creeks with spring outflows, in runs and pools.

CHARACTERISTICS:

(1) Mouth subterminal.

(2) Pharyngeal teeth 2,4-4,2 or 1,4-4,1.

(3) Black stripe on chin reaching to the isthmus.

(4) Membrane of dorsal fin with dark pigment distributed equally throughout fin; may be faded or absent on juveniles or females.

(5) Lateral line with 34–36 scales.

(6) Black midlateral stripe; may not be notable on all specimens.

(7) Purple, triangle-shaped bar above pectoral fins; most notable on breeding males.

DIMENSIONS: Up to 3 in (76 mm).

FIN COUNTS: Anal soft fin rays 8; pectoral soft fin rays 13.

COLORATION: Black stripe on chin reaching to the isthmus. Dorsal region olive to blue; lateral region silver with a black midlateral stripe. Fins of nonbreeding males are yellow to orange. Breeding males have orange fins trimmed with white, and the head is yellow with a brassy tint. Purple, triangle-shaped bar above pectoral fin.

COMMENTS: This species is listed by the state as threatened.

Blacktail shiner,
Cyprinella venusta,
4 in (102 mm)

Blacktail Shiner

Cyprinella venusta Girard, 1856

RANGE: Red River south and west to the Rio Grande basin.
HABITAT: Rivers and creeks in pools and runs.
CHARACTERISTICS:
(1) Snout pointed.
(2) Mouth terminal.
(3) Pharyngeal teeth 1,4-4,1 or 2,4-4,2
(4) Dark middorsal stripe present.
(5) Dorsal fin membrane with dark pigment concentrated posteriorly.
(6) Lateral line: 36–43 scales.
(7) Large, black caudal spot.
DIMENSIONS: Up to 7.5 in (191 mm).
FIN COUNTS: Anal soft fin rays 8–9; dorsal soft fin rays 8; pectoral soft fin rays 13–17; pelvic soft fin rays 8.
COLORATION: Dorsal region dark olive with dark middorsal stripe; lateral region silver-white with large, black caudal spot; ventral region white. Breeding males have blue dorsal and lateral regions with fins yellow-white.
COMMENTS: Female blacktail shiners have been observed emitting sounds to "call" males. Despite this unique call, this species will hybridize with red shiners.

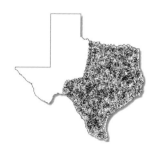

Common carp,
Cyprinus carpio,
10 in (254 mm)

Common Carp

Cyprinus carpio Linnaeus, 1758

RANGE: Statewide; introduced.

HABITAT: Lakes, ponds, rivers, and creeks in pools.

CHARACTERISTICS:

(1) Mouth subterminal; may be terminal on juveniles.

(2) Pharyngeal teeth 1,1,3-3,1,1 and molarlike.

(3) Upper jaw with two pairs of barbels.

(4) Dorsal fin with more than 15 soft dorsal rays.

(5) Dorsal and anal fins with single strong, serrated, hardened ray; 2 smaller hardened rays anterior to serrated ray.

(6) Lateral line scales: 35–38.

DIMENSIONS: Up to 48 in (1.2 m) and 60 lbs (27.2 kg).

FIN COUNTS: Anal soft fin rays 5–6; dorsal soft fin rays 17–21.

COLORATION: Dorsal region olive to gray; lateral region yellow-gold with silvery sheen; ventral region pale yellow. Dorsal and caudal fins gold-olive; other fins yellowish. Breeding males have a darker shade of the colors mentioned above with orange-gold fins. Juveniles have a dark vertical bar on caudal fin base.

COMMENTS: Morphologically distinct forms of common carp include the mirror carp, which has only a few large scales, and leather carp, which lacks scales entirely. The common carp is considered a nuisance because of its tendency to stir up sediments while feeding, which increases the water's turbidity and decreases the growth of phytoplankton and aquatic plants as well as suffocating fish eggs with sediments.

Manantial round-
nose minnow,
Dionda argentosa,
2.3 in (58 mm)

Manantial Roundnose Minnow

Dionda argentosa Girard, 1856

RANGE: Rio Grande drainage: Devils River, San Felipe Creek, and Sycamore Creek.

HABITAT: Rivers and creeks in runs and pools.

CHARACTERISTICS:

(1) Subterminal mouth.

(2) Pharyngeal teeth 0,4-4,0.

(3) Dark middorsal stripe.

(4) Black midlateral stripe from tip of snout ending just before a round caudal spot; may be absent on juveniles.

(5) Long, coiled intestine.

(6) Small, black, round caudal spot.

DIMENSIONS: Up to 2.5 in (64 mm).

FIN COUNTS: Anal soft fin rays 8.

COLORATION: Dorsal to midlateral region green-yellow; black midlateral stripe from tip of snout and ending just before a small, black, round caudal spot; lower lateral and ventral region silver-white or green.

COMMENTS: Feeds on algae and other vegetation; plant material in the gut gives the ventral region a dark green coloration.

Devils River minnow,
Dionda diaboli, 2 in
(51 mm)

Devils River Minnow
Dionda diaboli Hubbs and Brown, 1957

RANGE: Rio Grande drainage: Devils River and San Felipe Creek.
HABITAT: Rivers and creeks in runs and pools.
CHARACTERISTICS:
(1) Small, subterminal mouth.
(2) Pharyngeal teeth 0,4-4,0.
(3) Dorsal and lateral scales outlined with dark pigment.
(4) Dark midlateral stripe from tip of snout ending just before a wedge-shaped caudal spot. Stripe may be faded or absent.
(5) Row of double dashes formed by dark pigment above and below each lateral line pore; may be absent.
(6) Small, black, wedge-shaped caudal spot; may be absent on juveniles.
DIMENSIONS: Up to 2.5 in (64mm).
FIN COUNTS: Anal soft fin rays 8.
COLORATION: Dorsal region olive and scales edged with dark pigment; lateral region silver with scales edged with dark pigment; dark midlateral stripe from tip of snout ending just before a wedge-shaped caudal spot. Row of double dashes formed by dark pigment above and below each lateral line pore.
COMMENTS: The Devils River minnow can be distinguished from other roundnose minnow species by its dorsal and lateral scales outlined by melanophores and wedge-shaped caudal spot. This species is listed by the state as threatened.

Roundnose minnow,
Dionda episcopa,
2.5 in (64 mm)

Roundnose Minnow

Dionda episcopa Girard, 1856

RANGE: Rio Grande and Pecos River basins.

HABITAT: Headwaters, rivers, and creeks in pools and runs.

CHARACTERISTICS:

(1) Snout round.

(2) Pharyngeal teeth 0,4–4,0.

(3) Mouth subterminal.

(4) Dark middorsal stripe.

(5) Black midlateral stripe from tip of snout terminates just before a round caudal spot.

(6) Lateral line scales: 34–45.

(7) Long, coiled intestine.

(8) Small, black, round caudal spot.

DIMENSIONS: Up to 3 in (76 mm).

FIN COUNTS: Anal soft fin rays 8.

COLORATION: Dark middorsal stripe; dorsal to midlateral region green-yellow with black midlateral stripe from tip of snout and ending just before a small, black, round caudal spot; lower lateral and ventral region silver-white or green.

COMMENTS: Feeds on algae and other vegetation, which sometimes gives the ventral region a dark green coloration.

Guadalupe round-
nose minnow,
*Dionda nigrotae-
niata,* 2.5 in
(64 mm)

Guadalupe Roundnose Minnow

Dionda nigrotaeniata (Cope, 1880)

RANGE: Colorado and Guadalupe river basins.
HABITAT: Headwaters, creeks, and rivers in pools and runs.
CHARACTERISTICS:
(1) Snout round.
(2) Pharyngeal teeth 0,4-4,0.
(3) Mouth subterminal.
(4) Dark middorsal stripe.
(5) Black midlateral stripe from tip of snout ending just before a small caudal spot.
(6) Long, tightly coiled intestine.
(7) Small, black, round caudal spot.

DIMENSIONS: Up to 3 in (76 mm).
FIN COUNTS: Anal soft fin rays 8.
COLORATION: Dark middorsal stripe; dorsal to midlateral region yellow-green with black midlateral stripe from tip of snout ending just before a small, black, round caudal spot; lower lateral and ventral region silver-white or green.
COMMENTS: Feeds on algae and other vegetation, which sometimes gives the ventral region a dark green coloration.

Nueces roundnose minnow, *Dionda serena,*
1.8 in (46 mm)

Nueces Roundnose Minnow

Dionda serena Girard, 1856

RANGE: Nueces River basin.

HABITAT: Headwaters, creeks, and rivers in pools and runs.

CHARACTERISTICS:

(1) Snout round.

(2) Pharyngeal teeth 0,4-4,0.

(3) Mouth subterminal.

(4) Dark middorsal stripe.

(5) Black midlateral stripe from tip of snout ending just before a small caudal spot.

(6) Long, coiled intestine.

(7) Small, black, round caudal spot.

DIMENSIONS: Up to 3 in (76 mm).

FIN COUNTS: Anal soft fin rays 7.

COLORATION: Dark middorsal stripe; dorsal to midlateral region yellow-green with black; midlateral stripe from tip of snout ending just before a small, black, round caudal spot; lower lateral and ventral region silver-white or green.

COMMENTS: Feeds on algae and other vegetation, sometimes giving the ventral region a dark green coloration.

Preserved Rio Grande silvery minnow, *Hybognathus amarus,* 2.4 in (61 mm)

Rio Grande Silvery Minnow

Hybognathus amarus (Girard, 1856)

RANGE: Rio Grande and Pecos River basins; thought to be extirpated from these areas.

HABITAT: Rivers and creeks.

CHARACTERISTICS:

(1) Mouth subterminal.

(2) Pharyngeal teeth 0,4-4,0.

(3) Snout rounded; overhangs mouth slightly.

(4) Dark, broad middorsal stripe (one scale wide).

(5) Lateral line scales: 34–40.

(6) Intestine long and coiled.

(7) Black peritoneum (body cavity).

DIMENSIONS: Up to 3.5 in (89 mm).

FIN COUNTS: Anal soft fin rays 7–8; dorsal soft fin rays 7–9; pectoral soft fin rays 14–18.

COLORATION: Dark, broad midlateral stripe. Dorsal and lateral region silvery; ventral region white. Fins are colorless.

COMMENTS: This species is listed by the state as endangered.

Cypress minnow,
*Hybognathus
hayi,* 2.5 in
(64 mm)

Cypress Minnow

Hybognathus hayi (Jordan, 1885)

RANGE: Sabine River and Cypress Creek basins.

HABITAT: Rivers and streams with oxbow lakes, swamps, pools, and backwaters.

CHARACTERISTICS:

(1) Mouth large, oblique, and almost terminal.

(2) Snout broad and round; snout length less than eye diameter.

(3) Pharyngeal teeth 0,4-4,0.

(4) Thin, dark middorsal stripes (3); may be absent.

(5) Upper dorsal region with scales outlined by dark pigmentation.

(6) Lateral line scales: 35–41.

(7) Intestine long and coiled.

DIMENSIONS: Up to 4.5 in (120 mm).

FIN COUNTS: Anal soft fin rays 8; dorsal soft fin rays 8; pectoral soft fin rays 14–16.

COLORATION: Dorsal region olive with scales outlined by dark pigmentation; lateral region silver; ventral region white.

Mississippi silvery minnow, *Hybognathus nuchalis,* 4 in (102 mm)

Mississippi Silvery Minnow

Hybognathus nuchalis Agassiz, 1855

RANGE: Brazos River basin north and eastward to the Red River.
HABITAT: Rivers and creeks in pools and backwaters.
CHARACTERISTICS:
(1) Mouth subterminal.
(2) Pharyngeal teeth 0,4-4,0.
(3) Eyes large, with diameter going approximately 3.5–4.0 times into head length.
(4) Snout pointed; overhangs mouth slightly.
(5) Dark, broad middorsal stripe (one-half scale wide).
(6) dark pigment forms faint mid-

lateral stripe that becomes thinner and more notable posteriorly.
(7) Long, coiled intestine.
(8) Black peritoneum (body cavity).
(9) Lateral line scales: 34–40.
DIMENSIONS: Up to 7 in (178 mm).
FIN COUNTS: Anal soft fin rays 8; dorsal soft fin rays 8; pectoral soft fin rays 15–16; pelvic soft fin rays 8.
COLORATION: Dorsal region olive to gray with dark, broad middorsal stripe (one-half scale wide); lateral region silvery with dark pigmentation forming a faint midlateral stripe that becomes most notable posteriorly; ventral region white. The fins are colorless. Breeding males have a light shade of yellow on the lower lateral regions and lower fins.
COMMENTS: The Mississippi silvery minnow differs from the plains minnow in having larger eyes and scales.

Plains minnow,
Hybognathus
placitus, male,
3.2 in (81 mm)

Plains minnow,
Hybognathus
placitus, female,
3 in (76 mm)

Plains Minnow

Hybognathus placitus Girard, 1856

RANGE: Canadian, Red, Colorado, and Brazos river basins.

HABITAT: Rivers and creeks in pools and runs.

CHARACTERISTICS:

(1) Mouth subterminal.

(2) Pharyngeal teeth 0,4-4,0.

(3) Dark middorsal stripe.

(4) Dark pigmentation forms faint midlateral stripe.

(5) Lateral line scales: 36–39.

(6) Long, coiled intestine.

DIMENSIONS: Up to 5 in (127 mm).

FIN COUNTS: Anal soft fin rays 8; dorsal soft fin rays 8; pectoral soft fin rays 16–17; pelvic soft fin rays 8.

COLORATION: Dorsal region brown to olive with dark middorsal stripe; lateral region silvery with melanophores forming a faint midlateral stripe; ventral region white to faint yellow. Fins are colorless.

COMMENTS: See Mississippi silvery minnow (*Hybognathus nuchalis*).

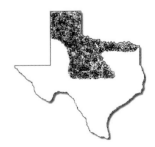

Pallid shiner,
Hybopsis amnis,
1.7 in (43 mm)

Pallid Shiner

Hybopsis amnis Hubbs and Greene,
1951

RANGE: Guadalupe River basin
eastward to the Sabine River basin.
HABITAT: Rivers and creeks with
pools.
CHARACTERISTICS:
(1) Blunt snout protruding over upper lip.
(2) Small, subterminal mouth, with
   upper jaw not reaching front of
   eye.
(3) Pharyngeal teeth 1,4-4,1.
(4) Upper jaw nearly hidden by suborbital bone when mouth is closed.
(5) Dark middorsal stripe.

(6) Dorsal fin, when folded against
   body, reaches to or past middle of
   anal fin base.
(7) Slender body.
(8) Black midlateral stripe (one scale
   wide) extending from tip of snout
   ending at a caudal spot; may be
   absent.
(9) Dorsal and anal fins slightly
   falcate (sickle shaped).
(10) Lateral line scales: 34–38.
(11) Faint caudal spot; may be absent.
DIMENSIONS: Up to 2.75 in
(70 mm)
FIN COUNTS: Anal soft fin rays
7–9; dorsal soft fin rays 8; pectoral
soft fin rays 12–15; pelvic soft fin
rays 8.
COLORATION: Dorsal region olive
with scales edged by faint pigmentation; lateral region silvery with black
midlateral stripe (one scale wide)
extending from tip of snout ending
at a faint caudal spot; ventral region
white.

Striped shiner, *Luxilus chrysocephalus,*
3.7 in (94 mm)

Striped Shiner

Luxilus chrysocephalus Rafinesque,
1820

RANGE: Northeastern portion of the
Red River basin.
HABITAT: Rivers and creeks in
pools.
CHARACTERISTICS:
(1) Mouth terminal and oblique.
(2) Pharyngeal teeth 2,4-4,2.
(3) Dark middorsal stripe.
(4) Dark pigment on chin.
(5) Dorsal region with stripes running horizontally and converging
at the midline of the dorsal region.
(6) Anterior lateral line scales taller
than wide (elevated).
(7) Midlateral region with dark
blotches; may be absent.
(8) Lateral line scales: 37–40.
DIMENSIONS: Up to 7 in
(178 mm).

FIN COUNTS: Anal soft fin rays
8–10; dorsal soft fin rays 8; pectoral
soft fin rays 15–17; pelvic soft fin
rays 8.
COLORATION: Dorsal region olive
with stripes running horizontally and
converging at the midline of the dorsal region; lateral region silver with
dark blotches, though blotches may
be absent; ventral region white. Fins
are colorless. Breeding males have
pink on head, body, and fins.

Ribbon shiner,
Lythrurus fumeus,
2.4 in (61 mm)

Ribbon Shiner

Lythrurus fumeus (Evermann, 1892)

RANGE: Lavaca River basin northward to the Red River basin and east to the Sabine River basin.

HABITAT: Headwaters, rivers, and creeks with pools.

CHARACTERISTICS:

(1) Snout pointed.

(2) Mouth terminal.

(3) Pharyngeal teeth usually 2,4-4,2.

(4) Dark pigment concentrated on chin.

(5) Crowded predorsal scales.

(6) Dark middorsal stripe.

(7) Dark pigment forms a midlateral stripe; may be absent.

(8) Lateral line scales: 35–45.

DIMENSIONS: Up to 2.8 in (71 mm).

FIN COUNTS: Anal soft fin rays 9–12; dorsal soft fin rays 8; pectoral soft fin rays 12–15; pelvic soft fin rays 8.

COLORATION: Dorsal region yellow-olive with dark middorsal stripe; lateral region silver; ventral region white. Fins are colorless. Breeding males have a yellow tint on body and yellow fins.

COMMENTS: The ribbon shiner may be distinguished from the redfin shiner (*Lythrurus umbratilis*) by the lack of a dark spot at the dorsal fin origin and dark dorsolateral chevron markings. The ribbon shiner may be distinguished from the emerald shiner (*Notropis atherinoides*) by crowded predorsal scales.

Redfin shiner,
Lythrurus umbratilis, 2.9 in
(74 mm)

Redfin Shiner
Lythrurus umbratilis (Girard, 1856)

RANGE: Red, Sabine, Neches, and Trinity river basins.

HABITAT: Headwaters, rivers, and creeks in pools.

CHARACTERISTICS:

(1) Mouth terminal.

(2) Pharyngeal teeth 2,4-4,2.

(3) Dark pigment concentrated on chin.

(4) Crowded predorsal scales.

(5) Dark chevron markings on anterior portion of lateral region; most notable on large specimens.

(6) Small, dark spot on anterior portion of dorsal fin base; most notable in adults.

(7) Dark middorsal stripe.

(8) Lateral line scales: 37–56, decurved.

DIMENSIONS: Up to 3.5 in (89 mm).

FIN COUNTS: Anal soft fin rays 10–12; dorsal soft fin rays 8; pectoral soft fin rays 12–13; pelvic soft fin rays 8.

COLORATION: Dorsal region blue to dark olive with dark middorsal stripe; lateral region silver with blue hue and dark chevron markings anteriorly; lower lateral region silvery white. Breeding males have blue-green dorsal and lateral regions with red fins.

COMMENTS: See ribbon shiner (*Lythrurus fumeus*).

Speckled chub,
*Macrhybopsis
aestivalis,* 2.5 in
(64 mm)

Speckled Chub

Macrhybopsis aestivalis (Girard, 1856)

RANGE: Rio Grande and Pecos River basins.

HABITAT: Rivers and creeks in runs.

CHARACTERISTICS:

(1) Eyes round.

(2) Snout round and blunt.

(3) Mouth inferior.

(4) Pharyngeal teeth 0,4-4,0.

(5) One pair of barbels.

(6) Lateral line scales: 31–42.

(7) Black spots scattered about lateral region.

DIMENSIONS: Up to 3 in (76 mm).

FIN COUNTS: Anal fin rays 7–9; dorsal fin rays 8; pectoral fin rays 11–18; pelvic fin rays 6–9.

COLORATION: Dorsal region olive to yellow with silver; lateral region silvery with black spots; ventral region white.

Shoal chub,
*Macrhybopsis
hyostoma*, 2.7 in
(69 mm)

Shoal Chub

Macrhybopsis hyostoma (Girard, 1884)

RANGE: Colorado River basin northeast to the Red River.

HABITAT: Rivers and creeks in riffles.

CHARACTERISTICS:

(1) Eyes small and round to large and oval shaped.

(2) Snout rounded.

(3) Mouth subterminal.

(4) Pharyngeal teeth 0,4-4,0 or 1,4-4,1.

(5) One or two pairs of barbels.

(6) Dark pigment might form a faint midlateral stripe.

(7) Lateral line scales: 32–43.

(8) Black spots scattered about lateral region.

DIMENSIONS: Up to 3 in (76 mm).

FIN COUNTS: Anal fin rays 7–10; dorsal fin rays 8; pectoral fin rays 11–18; pelvic fin rays 6–9.

COLORATION: Dorsal region green to gray; lateral region silvery with black spots, with melanophores possibly forming a faint midlateral stripe; ventral region silver-white.

Burrhead chub,
*Macrhybopsis
marconis*, 2.4 in
(61 mm)

Burrhead Chub

Macrhybopsis marconis (Jordan and
Gilbert, 1886)

RANGE: Guadalupe River basin.
HABITAT: Rivers and creeks in runs.
CHARACTERISTICS:
(1) Eyes large and round.
(2) Snout round.
(3) Mouth subterminal.
(4) Pharyngeal teeth 0,4-4,0 or
     1,4-4,1.
(5) One pair of barbels.
(6) Dark pigmentation forms a mid-
     lateral stripe.
(7) Lateral line scales: 38–41.
(8) Black spots scattered about lateral
     region.

DIMENSIONS: Up to 3 in (76 mm).
FIN COUNTS: Anal fin rays 7–9;
dorsal fin rays 8; pectoral fin rays
12–16; pelvic fin rays 8–9.
COLORATION: Dorsal region olive
to yellow with silver; lateral region
silvery with black spots, with melanophores forming a midlateral stripe;
ventral region white.

Silver chub,
*Macrhybopsis
storeriana,* 2.5 in
(64 mm)

Silver Chub

Macrhybopsis storeriana (Kirtland,
1845)

RANGE: Red River basin and the
lower Brazos River.

HABITAT: Lakes, rivers, and creeks
in pools and backwaters.

CHARACTERISTICS:

(1) Snout rounded.

(2) Mouth subterminal.

(3) Pharyngeal teeth 1,4-4,1.

(4) Small barbels in grooves at corners of mouth.

(5) Melanophores form a faint midlateral stripe; may be absent.

(6) Lateral line scales: 36–41.

DIMENSIONS: Up to 9 in
(228 mm).

FIN COUNTS: Anal soft fin rays 8;
dorsal soft fin rays 8; pectoral soft fin
rays 15–19; pelvic soft fin rays 8.

COLORATION: Dorsal region light
olive; lateral region silver-white;
ventral region white. The fins are colorless except for the caudal fin. The
edge of the lower lobe of the caudal
fin has a milky white coloration, and
thus the lower lobe edge stands out, a
feature most notable on large adults.

Peppered chub, *Macrhybopsis tetranema*, 2.8 in (71 mm)

Peppered Chub

Macrhybopsis tetranema (Gilbert, 1886)

RANGE: Portions of the Canadian River basin.
HABITAT: Rivers and creeks in runs.
CHARACTERISTICS:
(1) Eyes small.
(2) Snout pointed.
(3) Head conical.
(4) Mouth inferior.
(5) Two pairs of barbels.
(6) Dorsal fin origin ahead of pelvic fin insertion.
(7) Lateral line scales: 35–48.
(8) Pectoral fins falcate (sickle shaped) on males or pointed on females.
(9) Pharyngeal teeth 0,4-4,0.
(10) Black spots scattered over lateral region.
DIMENSIONS: Up to 3 in (76 mm)
FIN COUNTS: Anal soft fin rays 8.
COLORATION: Dorsal region olive to yellow with silver; lateral region silvery with black spots; ventral region white.

Golden shiner, *Notemigonus crysoleucas,* 2.3 in (58 mm)

Golden Shiner

Notemigonus crysoleucas (Mitchill, 1814)

RANGE: Statewide; introduced by bait bucket releases.

HABITAT: Lakes and swamps as well as rivers and creeks with pools and backwaters.

CHARACTERISTICS:

(1) Snout pointed.

(2) Mouth superior.

(3) Pharyngeal teeth 0,4-4,0 or 0,5-5,0.

(4) Lateral line scales: 44–54, greatly decurved.

(5) Black midlateral stripe from tip of snout to caudal fin base; faded or absent on adults.

(6) Ventral region behind pelvic fins with a fleshy midventral keel with scales not overlapping keel.

DIMENSIONS: Up to 12 in (305 mm).

FIN COUNTS: Anal soft fin rays 8–19; dorsal soft fin rays 7–9; pectoral soft fin rays 15–18.

COLORATION: Dorsal region gold with olive green; lateral region silver or gold, with black midlateral stripe from snout to caudal fin base; ventral region pale yellow. Fins are yellow or light orange.

Texas shiner,
Notropis amabilis,
2.4 in (63 mm)

Texas Shiner
Notropis amabilis (Girard, 1856)

RANGE: Basins of the Edwards Plateau to the Rio Grande.

HABITAT: Headwaters, creeks, and rivers in runs and pools.

CHARACTERISTICS:

(1) Eyes large; eye diameter greater than snout length.

(2) Black lips.

(3) Mouth terminal.

(4) Pharyngeal teeth 2,4-4,2.

(5) Dark middorsal stripe.

(6) Lateral line scales: 32–36.

DIMENSIONS: Up to 2.5 in (64 mm).

FIN COUNTS: Anal soft fin rays 6–8.

COLORATION: Dorsal region olive with dark middorsal stripe; lateral region silvery, with dorsal and upper lateral scales outlined in dark pigmentation; ventral region white.

Emerald shiner,
*Notropis atheri-
noides,* 2.5 in
(64 mm)

Emerald Shiner

Notropis atherinoides Rafinesque,
1818

RANGE: Canadian, Red, Sabine,
and Neches river basins as well as the
lower basin of the Trinity River.
HABITAT: Lakes and rivers in pools
and runs.
CHARACTERISTICS:
(1) Mouth terminal.
(2) Pharyngeal teeth 2,4-4,2.
(3) Dark pigment concentrated on
chin.
(4) Dark middorsal stripe.
(5) Dorsal fin origin well behind base
of pelvic fins.
(6) Lateral line scales: 35–40.
(7) Silver midlateral stripe; may be
absent.
DIMENSIONS: Up to 5 in
(127 mm).

FIN COUNTS: Anal soft fin rays
10–12; dorsal soft fin rays 8; pectoral
soft fin rays 13–17; pelvic soft fin
rays 8.
COLORATION: Dorsal region dark
olive and emerald with thin middorsal stripe; lateral region emerald
with silver midlateral stripe; ventral
region silvery white. Fins are white or
colorless.
COMMENTS: See ribbon shiner
(*Lythrurus fumeus*).

Blackspot shiner,
Notropis atrocaudalis, 2.7 in (69 mm)

Blackspot Shiner

Notropis atrocaudalis Evermann, 1892

RANGE: Brazos River basin and north to the Red River and east to the Sabine River.

HABITAT: Rivers and creeks in runs and pools.

CHARACTERISTICS:

(1) Snout rounded.

(2) Mouth subterminal.

(3) Pharyngeal teeth 0,4-4,0.

(4) Dark middorsal stripe.

(5) Black midlateral stripe (about width of eye) from tip of snout to terminate at a small, rectangular caudal spot.

(6) Lateral line scales: 35–40.

(7) Pigmentation of upper lateral and dorsal scale edges forms horizontal stripes.

(8) Small, black, rectangular caudal spot, with pigmentation running onto caudal fin; in some juvenile specimens there might be a space between midlateral stripe and caudal spot.

DIMENSIONS: Up to 3 in (76 mm).

FIN COUNTS: Anal soft fin rays 8.

COLORATION: Dorsal and upper lateral regions olive with dark middorsal stripe; lateral region silvery with a thin, dark midlateral stripe from snout to small, black, rectangular caudal spot (pigmentation runs onto caudal fin); lower lateral and ventral region white.

Red River shiner, *Notropis bairdi,* 1.7 in (43 mm)

Red River Shiner
Notropis bairdi Hubbs and
Ortenburger, 1929

RANGE: Red River basin.
HABITAT: River channels.
CHARACTERISTICS:
(1) Broad, flat head.
(2) Large mouth, nearly terminal.
(3) Pharyngeal teeth 0,4-4,0.
(4) Snout conical.
(5) Eyes positioned high on head.
(6) Small area of anterior portion of
nape lacks scales.
(7) Dark middorsal stripe.
(8) Lateral line interrupted; 33–37
scales.
(9) Breast partly unscaled.
DIMENSIONS: Up to 3.25 in
(83 mm).

FIN COUNTS: Anal soft fin rays 7;
dorsal soft fin rays 8; pectoral soft fin
rays 15.
COLORATION: Dorsal region tan to
gray with thin, dark middorsal stripe
and scales outlined by melanophores;
lateral and ventral region silver.

Tamaulipas shiner, *Notropis braytoni,* 1.5 in (38 mm)

Tamaulipas Shiner

Notropis braytoni Jordan and Evermann, 1896

RANGE: Rio Grande basin.
HABITAT: River and creek channels.
CHARACTERISTICS:
(1) Snout rounded.
(2) Mouth subterminal.
(3) Pharyngeal teeth 1,4-4,1.
(4) Dark, middorsal stripe.
(5) Dark pigment forms midlateral stripe, which is scattered anteriorly and concentrated posteriorly, ending just before a small, black caudal spot.
(6) Lateral line scales: 32–39.
(7) Small, black caudal spot.

DIMENSIONS: Up to 2.8 in (71 mm).
FIN COUNTS: Anal soft fin rays 7; dorsal soft fin rays 15–16.
COLORATION: Dorsal region light olive with dark, middorsal stripe; lateral region silver with dark pigment forming a midlateral stripe, which is scattered anteriorly and concentrated posteriorly, ending just before a small, black caudal spot; ventral region white.

Smalleye shiner, *Notropis buccula,*
1.5 in (38 mm)

Smalleye Shiner

Notropis buccula Cross, 1953

RANGE: Sections of the Brazos
River basin; may also be encountered
in the Colorado River near Austin,
Texas, as a result of introductions.
HABITAT: River channels.
CHARACTERISTICS:
(1) Mouth subterminal.
(2) Snout long; snout length greater
than distance from anterior tip
of mandible to posterior tip of
maxillary.
(3) Lateral line scales: 33–37.
(4) Nape and breast partly scaled.
(5) Dark pigment forms midlateral
stripe that is scattered anteriorly
and concentrated posteriorly.
DIMENSIONS: Up to 1.7 in
(44 mm).
FIN COUNTS: Anal soft fin rays 7;
dorsal fin rays 8; pelvic fin rays 8.

COLORATION: Dorsal region olive-
green with scales outlined by dark
pigment; lateral region silver with
melanophores forming midlateral
stripe that is scattered anteriorly and
concentrated posteriorly; ventral
region white.
COMMENTS: The smalleye shiner
may be distinguished from the Red
River shiner by its longer snout.

Ghost shiner, *Notropis buchanani,* 1.3 in (33 mm)

Ghost Shiner

Notropis buchanani Meek, 1896

RANGE: Lower Rio Grande basin northward to the Red River.

HABITAT: Rivers and creeks in pools and backwaters.

CHARACTERISTICS:

(1) Snout rounded.

(2) Incomplete infraorbital canal.

(3) Pharyngeal teeth 0,4-4,0.

(4) First few anterior lateral line scales taller than wide (elevated).

(5) Lateral line scales: 30–35.

(6) Dark pigment forms faint midlateral stripe on the posterior area of the lateral region; may be absent.

A silver midlateral stripe may be notable.

(7) Dark pigment at base of anal fin forms midventral line that continues to caudal fin.

DIMENSIONS: Up to 2.5 in (64 mm).

FIN COUNTS: Anal soft fin rays 8; pectoral soft fin rays 13–15.

COLORATION: Dorsal region white; specimens from clear water may have scale edges slightly pigmented; lateral region white with dark pigmentation forming faint midlateral stripe on the posterior area of the lateral region (silver midlateral stripe may be notable); ventral region white with dark pigmentation on anal fin base forming midventral line to caudal fin.

COMMENTS: The ghost shiner can be distinguished from the mimic shiner by the former's incomplete infraorbital canal in the cephalic lateral line and little to no pigment on the body.

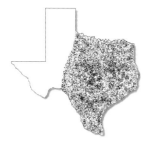

Ironcolor shiner,
Notropis chaly-baeus, 2 in
(51 mm)

Ironcolor Shiner
Notropis chalybaeus (Cope, 1867)

RANGE: Sabine River northeast to the Red River basin, with a disjunct population in the upper reaches of the San Marcos River.

HABITAT: Rivers and creeks in pools and runs.

CHARACTERISTICS:

(1) Interior of mouth with dark pigmentation.

(2) Pharyngeal teeth 2,4-4,2.

(3) Dark middorsal stripe.

(4) Dorsal scale edges outlined by melanophores; the scales just above midlateral stripe lack pigmentation, giving the appearance of a gold stripe.

(5) Lateral line scales: 33–37; lateral line may be incomplete in juvenile specimens.

(6) Black midlateral stripe from tip of snout ending in a weakly defined caudal spot; pigmentation may run onto caudal fin.

(7) Dark pigmentation on anal fin base forms midventral line that runs to caudal fin.

DIMENSIONS: Up to 2.5 in (64 mm).

FIN COUNTS: Anal soft fin rays 8; dorsal soft fin rays 8; pelvic soft fin rays 8.

COLORATION: Dorsal region faintly yellow with scale edges darkly pigmented and middorsal stripe present; upper lateral region gold, which forms a stripe just above midlateral stripe; lower lateral and ventral regions silver white, with black midlateral stripe from tip of snout ending in a weakly defined caudal spot (pigmentation might run onto caudal fin); pigmentation on anal fin base runs to caudal fin. Breeding male ironcolor shiners have an orange-gold body and fins.

Chihuahua shiner, *Notropis chihuahua,* 2.2 in (56 mm)

Chihuahua Shiner

Notropis chihuahua Woolman, 1892

RANGE: Rio Grande tributaries in the Big Bend region.

HABITAT: Rivers and creeks in pools and runs.

CHARACTERISTICS:

(1) Snout rounded.

(2) Pharyngeal teeth 0,4-4,0 or 1,4-4,1.

(3) Dark middorsal stripe.

(4) Dark spots on dorsal and lateral region.

(5) Lateral line scales: 33–37.

(6) Dark pigment forms faint midlateral stripe; may be absent.

(7) Small, black, wedge-shaped caudal spot.

DIMENSIONS: Up to 3.3 in (84 mm).

FIN COUNTS: Anal soft fin rays 7–8.

COLORATION: Dorsal region pale olive with dark spots and dark middorsal stripe; lateral region silver with dark spots, a black wedge-shaped caudal spot, and dark pigment forming a faint midlateral stripe; ventral region white. Fins are pale yellow to orange, excluding pelvic fins.

COMMENTS: This species is listed by the state as threatened.

Arkansas River shiner, *Notropis girardi,* 1.3 in (33 mm)

Arkansas River Shiner

Notropis girardi Hubbs and Ortenburger, 1829

RANGE: Canadian River basin.

HABITAT: Rivers and creeks.

CHARACTERISTICS:

(1) Head small, dorsally flattened; head length approximately 4.3 times into standard length.

(2) Snout rounded.

(3) Pharyngeal teeth 0,4-4,0.

(4) Small eyes; eye diameter 4.5 times or more into head length.

(5) Dorsal fin tall; anterior dorsal fin rays reach past posterior rays when dorsal fin is folded down.

(6) Pectoral fins long and falcate (sickle shaped) in males, rounded in females.

(7) Lateral line scales: 32–37.

(8) Small, dark chevron marking at base of caudal fin.

DIMENSIONS: Up to 2 in (51 mm).

FIN COUNTS: Anal soft fin rays 8; pectoral soft fin rays 14; pelvic soft fin rays 8.

COLORATION: Dorsal region tan with scales outlined by dark pigment; lateral region silver with first few lateral line pores outlined by dark pigment, which may be absent; ventral region white. Small, dark chevron marking at base of caudal fin.

COMMENTS: This species is listed by the state as threatened.

Rio Grande
shiner, *Notropis
jemezanus,*
1.25 in (32 mm)

Rio Grande Shiner

Notropis jemezanus (Cope, 1875)

RANGE: Rio Grande basin.
HABITAT: Rivers and creeks with
runs and pools.
CHARACTERISTICS:
(1) Eye diameter is equal to or less
than snout length.
(2) Mouth large and terminal.
(3) Chin and lower lip with scattered
dark pigment. Pigmentation, if
any, is not as dark as that found on
Texas shiners (*Notropis amabalis*).
(4) Pharyngeal teeth 2,4-4,2.
(5) Thin, dark middorsal line, 1 to 2
melanophores wide.

(6) Lateral region with dark midlateral stripe; may not be notable on
all specimens.
(7) Pelvic fins short; when depressed
against body do not reach to anus.
(8) Lateral line scales: fewer than 40.
DIMENSIONS: Up to 3 in (76 mm).
FIN COUNTS: Anal soft fin rays
9–11; dorsal soft fin rays 7–8; pectoral soft fin rays 14–15; pelvic soft fin
rays 8.
COLORATION: Dorsal region olive
with thin, dark middorsal line; lateral
region silver with dark midlateral
stripe that may not be notable on
all specimens; ventral region silver-
white.
COMMENTS: Rio Grande shiners
can be distinguished from Texas shiners (*Notropis amabalis*) by their
smaller eyes, short pectoral fins,
and lack of black pigmentation on
lower lip.

Taillight shiner,
Notropis maculatus,
breeding male,
1 in (25 mm)

Taillight Shiner

Notropis maculatus (Hay, 1881)

RANGE: Sulphur and Cypress creek drainages.

HABITAT: Swamps and ponds as well as creeks in backwaters and pools.

CHARACTERISTICS:

(1) Snout rounded.

(2) Mouth subterminal.

(3) Pharyngeal teeth 0,4-4,0.

(4) Dorsal and upper lateral scale edges outlined with dark pigment.

(5) Dark middorsal stripe.

(6) Black spot on midanterior portion of dorsal fin; most notable on adults and may be absent on juveniles.

(7) Lateral line incomplete: 34–39 scales.

(8) Black midlateral stripe from the tip of the snout ending just before a large caudal spot; stripe may be faded or absent.

(9) Black, round caudal spot and two smaller triangle-shaped spots with one above and one below caudal spot.

DIMENSIONS: Up to 3 in (76 mm).

FIN COUNTS: Anal soft fin rays 8; dorsal soft fin rays 8; pectoral soft fin rays 13–15.

COLORATION: Dorsal region light olive with thin, dark middorsal stripe; lateral region silver with black midlateral stripe ending just before a large, dark, round caudal spot, with smaller dark triangular spots above and below caudal spot; ventral region white. Breeding males have a red body and fins with red-and-black edges.

Sharpnose shiner,
Notropis oxyrhynchus,
1.5 in (38 mm)

Sharpnose Shiner

Notropis oxyrhynchus Hubbs and
Bonham, 1951

RANGE: Brazos River basin. A population of sharpnose shiners in the
Colorado River above Lake Buchanan
is thought to have been introduced.

HABITAT: Rivers in runs and pools.

CHARACTERISTICS:
(1) Snout sharply pointed.
(2) Pharyngeal teeth 2,4-4,2.
(3) Dark middorsal stripe; may be
absent.
(4) Lateral line scales: 34–37, slightly
decurved.
(5) Melanophores on anal fin base.

DIMENSIONS: Up to 2.5 in
(64 mm).

FIN COUNTS: Anal soft fin rays 10.

COLORATION: Dorsal region dark
olive with dark middorsal stripe; lateral region silver with melanophores
forming faint midlateral stripe, most
notable posteriorly; ventral region
silver- white with pigmentation on
anal fin base.

COMMENTS: Considered threatened by Hubbs et al. (1991).

Chub shiner,
Notropis potteri,
3 in (76 mm)

Chub Shiner

Notropis potteri Hubbs and Bonham, 1951

RANGE: Brazos and Red Rivers, as well as a portion of the San Jacinto River basin.

HABITAT: Rivers in runs and riffles.

CHARACTERISTICS:

(1) Small eyes, positioned high on head.

(2) Head flat and wide.

(3) Posterior portion of upper lip swollen.

(4) Median portion of lower lip swollen.

(5) Pharyngeal teeth 2,4-4,2 or 1,4-4,1.

(6) Dark pigment forms a faint mid-lateral stripe; may be absent.

(7) Small, black, round caudal spot; may be absent.

DIMENSIONS: Up to 3.5 in (89 mm).

FIN COUNTS: Anal soft fin rays 7; dorsal soft fin rays 8.

COLORATION: Dorsal region yellow-olive; lateral region silvery with dark pigment forming a faint mid-lateral stripe; ventral region silver-white.

Sabine shiner, *Notropis sabinae,* 1.7 in (43 mm)

Sabine Shiner

Notropis sabinae, Jordan and Gilbert, 1886

RANGE: San Jacinto River basin to the Sabine River basin.

HABITAT: Rivers and creeks in pools and runs.

CHARACTERISTICS:

(1) Snout rounded.

(2) Eyes positioned high on head.

(3) Mouth subterminal.

(4) Pharyngeal teeth 0,4–4,0 or 1,4–4,1.

(5) Ventral surface of head flat.

(6) Lateral line scales: 31–37.

(7) Dark middorsal stripe.

DIMENSIONS: Up to 2.3 in (58 mm).

FIN COUNTS: Anal soft fin rays 7.

COLORATION: Dorsal region olive-yellow with dark middorsal stripe; lateral region silver; ventral region white.

Silverband shiner, *Notropis shumardi*, 2.7 in (69 mm)

Silverband Shiner

Notropis shumardi, (Baird and Girard, 1856)

RANGE: Brazos River basin and southward to the Lavaca River basin. This species can also be found in the Red and Trinity river basins.

HABITAT: Rivers in pools and runs.

CHARACTERISTICS:

(1) Snout pointed.

(2) Mouth terminal.

(3) Pharyngeal teeth 2,4-4,2.

(4) Dark middorsal stripe.

(5) Lateral line scales: 33–39.

(6) Silver midlateral stripe.

DIMENSIONS: Up to 4 in (102 mm).

FIN COUNTS: Anal soft fin rays 8–9; pelvic soft fin rays 9.

COLORATION: Dorsal region light olive with middorsal stripe; lateral region silver with silver midlateral stripe; ventral region white.

Sand shiner, *Notropis stramineus,* 2 in (51 mm)

Sand Shiner

Notropis stramineus (Cope, 1865)

RANGE: Edwards Plateau basins as well as portions of the Pecos River, Canadian, Red River, and Rio Grande (Big Bend) basins.

HABITAT: Lakes, rivers, and creeks in runs and pools.

CHARACTERISTICS:

(1) Mouth terminal and slightly oblique.

(2) Dark middorsal stripe.

(3) Pharyngeal teeth 0,4-4,0.

(4) When viewed from above, dorsal fin base has two dark dashes separated by a clear space.

(5) Dark pigment forms a row of double dashes along lateral line.

(6) Dark pigment forms midlateral stripe; most notable on caudal peduncle.

(7) Small, dark caudal spot; may be absent.

DIMENSIONS: Up to 3.2 in (81 mm).

FIN COUNTS: Anal soft fin rays 6–8; pectoral soft fin rays 13–15; pelvic soft fin rays 8.

COLORATION: Dorsal region olive-yellow with a dark middorsal stripe and scales outlined by dark pigment; lateral region silver with melanophores forming midlateral stripe that is most notable on caudal peduncle; ventral region silvery white. Fins are clear.

COMMENTS: A sand shiner may be distinguished from the mimic shiner and the ghost shiner by its lack of elevated (taller than wide) lateral line scales.

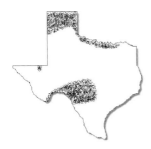

Weed shiner, *Notropis texanus,* 1.7 in (43 mm)

Weed Shiner

Notropis texanus (Girard, 1856)

RANGE: Nueces River basin northeast to the Red River.

HABITAT: Rivers and creeks in pools and runs.

CHARACTERISTICS:

(1) Snout rounded.

(2) Mouth terminal.

(3) Pharyngeal teeth 2,4-4,2.

(4) Dark middorsal stripe.

(5) Dorsal and upper lateral scale edges outlined by dark pigment.

(6) Black midlateral stripe from tip of snout ending into or just before, a caudal spot.

(7) Lateral line scales: 32–39.

(8) Small, black, rectangular caudal spot; pigmentation of caudal spot can run onto caudal fin.

DIMENSIONS: Up to 3.5 in (89 mm).

FIN COUNTS: Anal soft fin rays 6–8; pectoral soft fin rays 12–16; pelvic soft fin rays 8.

COLORATION: Dorsal region olive with middorsal stripe and scale edges outlined by dark pigment; lateral region has black midlateral stripe that runs from tip of snout to end in or just before a small, dark caudal spot; ventral region silvery white.

Mimic shiner, *Notropis volucellus,*
2.6 in (66 mm)

Mimic Shiner

Notropis volucellus (Cope, 1865)

RANGE: Nueces River basin north to
the Red River.
HABITAT: Lakes as well as headwaters, rivers, and creeks in pools.
CHARACTERISTICS:
(1) Snout rounded.
(2) Mouth subterminal.
(3) Pharyngeal teeth 0,4-4,0.
(4) Dark middorsal stripe.
(5) First few lateral line scales taller
than wide (elevated).
(6) Dark pigment forms faint midlateral stripe that ends in a small
triangle-shaped caudal spot.

(7) Lateral line scales: 32–38.
(8) Dark pigment on anal fin base
forms midventral stripe to caudal
fin.
(9) Small, dark, triangle-shaped caudal spot.
DIMENSIONS: Up to 3 in (76 mm).
FIN COUNTS: Anal soft fin rays 8;
pectoral soft fin rays 13–17; pelvic
soft fin rays 8.
COLORATION: Dorsal region olive-
yellow with dark middorsal stripe;
lateral region silver with dark pigment
forming a faint midlateral stripe ending in a small, dark, triangular caudal
spot; ventral region white with anal
fin base pigmentation forming midventral line running to caudal fin.
COMMENTS: The mimic shiner can
be distinguished from the ghost
shiner by its complete infraorbital
canal and greater pigmentation of
the body.

Pugnose minnow, *Opso-poeodus emiliae*, 2.3 in (58 mm)

Pugnose Minnow

Opsopoeodus emiliae Hay, 1881

RANGE: Nueces River basin northeastward to the Red River.

HABITAT: Swamps, oxbows, rivers, creeks and lakes.

CHARACTERISTICS:

(1) Snout rounded.

(2) Mouth small, superior.

(3) Pharyngeal teeth 0,5-5,0.

(4) Dorsal and upper lateral scale edges outlined by melanophores.

(5) Predorsal scales crowded.

(6) Anterior and posterior rays of dorsal fin pigmented; most notable on males.

(7) Black midlateral stripe from tip of snout ends at caudal fin base; the stripe is most notable on juveniles and faded on adults.

(8) Lateral line scales: 36–42; lateral line may be incomplete.

(9) Small, black caudal spot with some pigmentation running onto the caudal fin.

DIMENSIONS: Up to 2.5 in (64 mm).

FIN COUNTS: Anal soft fin rays 8; dorsal soft fin rays 9; pectoral soft fin rays 13–16.

COLORATION: Dorsal region yellow-silver with scale edges outlined by melanophores; lateral region silver with black midlateral stripe from tip of snout to caudal fin base that may terminate just before a small black caudal spot; pigmentation may run onto caudal fin; ventral region silver.

Suckermouth minnow, *Phenacobius mirabilis,* 2.7 in (69 mm)

Suckermouth Minnow
Phenacobius mirabilis (Girard, 1856)

RANGE: Colorado, Canadian, Red, Sabine, and Trinity river basins.

HABITAT: Rivers and creeks in riffles and runs.

CHARACTERISTICS:

(1) Snout rounded.

(2) Mouth subterminal.

(3) Pharyngeal teeth 0,4-4,0.

(4) Eyes positioned high on head.

(5) Large fleshy lips; lower lip forms lobes at corners of mouth.

(6) Dorsal and upper lateral scale edges outlined by dark pigment; may be absent.

(7) Dark middorsal stripe.

(8) Black midlateral stripe starting from head and ending in a small, black caudal spot; stripe may be faint on larger specimens or those taken from turbid water.

(9) Lateral line scales: 42–51.

(10) Small, black caudal spot.

DIMENSIONS: Up to 4.8 in (122 mm).

FIN COUNTS: Anal soft fin rays 7; dorsal soft fin rays 8; pectoral soft fin rays 13–16; pelvic soft fin rays 8.

COLORATION: Dorsal region olive-gray with thin, dark middorsal stripe; lateral region silvery with black midlateral stripe ending in a small, black caudal spot; ventral region silver-white.

Fathead minnow, *Pimephales promelas,* breeding male, 2.6 in (66 mm)

Fathead minnow, *Pimephales promelas,* nonbreeding adult, 1.7 in (43 mm)

Fathead Minnow

Pimephales promelas Rafinesque, 1820

RANGE: Statewide.

HABITAT: Ponds as well as head-waters, creeks, and rivers in pools.

CHARACTERISTICS:

(1) Snout blunt.

(2) Mouth terminal.

(3) Pharyngeal teeth 0,4–4,0.

(4) Dark middorsal stripe.

(5) Predorsal scales crowded.

(6) Chevron-type markings on upper anterior portion of lateral region; may be absent.

(7) Dark spot on midanterior portion of dorsal fin; may be absent on juveniles.

(8) Black midlateral stripe; faded on adults and those taken from turbid water.

(9) Lateral line scales: 40- 54, usually incomplete.

(10) Long intestine, more than twice the length of the body.

(11) Peritoneum (body cavity) black.

DIMENSIONS: Up to 4 in (102 mm).

FIN COUNTS: Anal soft fin rays 7; dorsal soft fin rays 8; pectoral soft fin rays 15–18; pelvic soft fin rays 8.

COLORATION: Dorsal region dark olive with dark middorsal stripe and pigmentation forming spot on mid-anterior portion of dorsal fin; lateral region olive with midlateral stripe and chevron-type markings on upper anterior portion, ventral region olive. Breeding males have black head and fins and dark body with two white or gold areas behind the head and under the dorsal fin.

COMMENTS: The thick predorsal pad on breeding males is thought to be for cleaning nesting sites (the underside of hard surfaces) and se-creting mucous to protect eggs against disease.

Bullhead minnow, *Pimephales vigilax,* 2.5 in (64 mm)

Bullhead Minnow

Pimephales vigilax (Baird and Girard)

RANGE: Statewide.

HABITAT: Rivers in pools and runs.

CHARACTERISTICS:

(1) Snout rounded.

(2) Mouth subterminal.

(3) Pharyngeal teeth 0,4-4,0.

(4) Predorsal scales crowded.

(5) Pigmentation forms spot on midanterior portion of dorsal fin; absent on juveniles.

(6) Pigmentation forms midlateral stripe with anterior portion narrow and posterior portion wide, ending just before a small, caudal spot; stripe may be absent.

(7) Lateral line scales: 37–47.

(8) Short intestine.

(9) Peritoneum (body cavity) silvery.

(10) Small, round caudal spot.

DIMENSIONS: Up to 3.5 in (89 mm).

FIN COUNTS: Anal soft fin rays 7; dorsal soft fin rays 8; pectoral soft fin rays 8; pelvic soft fin rays 15–16.

COLORATION: Dorsal region dark to light olive with pigmentation forming midanterior spot on dorsal fin; lateral region silvery with faint midlateral stripe, narrow anteriorly and wide posteriorly, ending just before a small, round caudal spot; ventral region silvery white. Breeding males have steel blue body and dark gray head with dorsal fin's first ray white and two dark blotches set off by white; caudal fin white anteriorly and dark gray posteriorly; pectoral fins with first one or two rays dark and remainder of fin white.

COMMENTS: The thick predorsal skin pad of breeding males is thought to be used for cleaning eggs (attached to the underside of hard surfaces).

Flathead chub, *Platy-gobio gracilis,* 6.3 in (160 mm)

Flathead Chub

Platygobio gracilis Richardson, 1836

RANGE: Canadian River basin.

HABITAT: Rivers in runs.

CHARACTERISTICS:

(1) Head broad and dorsally flat-tened.

(2) Eyes small.

(3) Mouth large and subterminal.

(4) One pair of small barbels.

(5) Snout pointed.

(6) Pharyngeal teeth 2,4-4,2.

(7) Pectoral fins falcate (sickle shaped).

(8) Lateral line scales: 42–59.

DIMENSIONS: Up to 12.5 in (318 mm)

FIN COUNTS: Anal soft fin rays 7–9; dorsal soft fin rays 8; pectoral soft fin rays; pelvic soft fin rays 8.

COLORATION: Dorsal region light brown; lateral and ventral regions silvery.

Bluehead shiner, *Pteronotropis hubbsi,* 6.7 in (170 mm)

Bluehead Shiner

Pteronotropis hubbsi (Bailey and Robison, 1978)

RANGE: Rivers and creeks in the vicinity of Caddo Lake.
HABITAT: Usually found in rivers and creeks with backwaters, oxbow lakes, and pools.
CHARACTERISTICS:
(1) Snout short and blunt.
(2) Mouth terminal, sharply upturned.
(3) Pharyngeal teeth 0,4-4,0.
(4) Top of head bright blue in breeding males only.
(5) Dorsal scale edges outlined by dark pigment; the scales just above midlateral stripe lack pigmentation, giving the appearance of a gold stripe.

(6) Dorsal fin origin behind pelvic fin insertion.
(7) Black midlateral stripe extends from tip of snout to a large caudal spot.
(8) Large dorsal and anal fins in breeding males only.
(9) Deep body.
(10) Lateral line incomplete; 34–38 lateral series scales.
DIMENSIONS: Up to 2.5 in (60 mm).
FIN COUNTS: Anal soft fin rays 11; dorsal soft fin rays 10.
COLORATION: Dorsal region faint yellow with scale edges darkly pigmented; gold upper lateral region that forms a stripe just above midlateral stripe; lower lateral and ventral regions silver-white; black midlateral stripe extending from tip of snout to a large caudal spot; pigmentation might run onto caudal fin. In breeding males dorsal region of head is bright blue and fins are orange.
COMMENTS: A bluehead shiner can be distinguished from an ironcolor shiner (*Notropis chalybaeus*) by its large caudal spot. The state considers this species threatened.

Longnose dace, *Rhinichthys cataractae,* 2 in (51 mm)

Longnose Dace
Rhinichthys cataractae (Valenciennes, 1842)

RANGE: Rio Grande basin.

HABITAT: Rocky lake shores and fast riffles (occasionally runs and pools).

CHARACTERISTICS:

(1) Snout long (hangs over lower lip 1–3 mm or more).

(2) Mouth subterminal.

(3) Pharyngeal teeth 2,4-4,2.

(4) Upper lip connected to snout by frenum.

(5) Barbels present (positioned in grooves at angles of mouth).

(6) Pigmentation forms spots and mottling on dorsal and lateral regions.

(7) Pigmentation forms midlateral band, which may be absent or faded in adults but notable on young.

(8) Small, dark basicaudal spot.

DIMENSIONS: Up to 6.3 in (160 mm).

FIN COUNTS: Anal soft fin rays 7–9 (usually 8); dorsal soft fin rays 8; pectoral soft fin rays 13–15.

COLORATION: Dorsal region green to brown (lake specimens gray) with dark spots and mottling; lateral region light green or brown with dark spots and mottling (pigmentation forms midlateral band terminating in a small, dark basicaudal spot; band is absent or faded in adults but notable in young); ventral region silvery white. Breeding males have head and fin bases colored bright red.

COMMENTS: The longnose dace is tolerant of rapid environmental changes, such as temperature fluctuation, turbidity, and short periods of low oxygen content.

Creek chub,
*Semotilus atro-
maculatus*, 6.7 in
(170 mm)

Creek Chub

Semotilus atromaculatus (Mitchill, 1818)

RANGE: East Texas and the lower portions of the Brazos River basin.
HABITAT: Headwaters and creeks.
CHARACTERISTICS:
(1) Snout pointed.
(2) Mouth large and terminal.
(3) Pharyngeal teeth 2,5-4,2.
(4) Small flat barbels positioned in groove above upper lip near posterior end of jaw, difficult to find in some specimens; may be absent.
(5) Predorsal scales crowded.
(6) Dark middorsal stripe.
(7) Dark pigmentation forms spot at dorsal fin base.
(8) Pigmentation forms midlateral stripe from snout ending in a small, wedge-shaped caudal spot; most notable on juveniles.

(9) Lateral line scales: 42–70.
(10) Small, wedge-shaped caudal spot.
DIMENSIONS: Up to 12 in (305 mm).
FIN COUNTS: Anal soft fin rays 8; dorsal soft fin rays 8; pectoral soft fin rays 13–18; pelvic soft fin rays 8.
COLORATION: Dorsal region dark olive with middorsal stripe; lateral region silver-green with pigmentation forming midlateral stripe from snout ending in a small, wedge-shaped caudal spot; ventral region white. The creek chub has yellow fins and black bar at posterior of operculum. Breeding males have orange on dorsal fin base and orange lower fins with blue on side of head and pink on lower half of head.
COMMENTS: During breeding the male digs a nest in gravel substrate by moving gravel with its mouth, after eggs have been laid, the male covers the eggs with gravel and proceeds to dig another nest just downstream from the buried eggs, repeating the process until there is a gravel ridge covering several clutches of eggs.

River carpsucker,
Carpiodes carpio,
9.2 in (234 mm)

River Carpsucker

Carpiodes carpio (Rafinesque, 1820)

RANGE: Statewide.

HABITAT: Lakes, creeks, and rivers.

CHARACTERISTICS:

(1) Snout pointed.

(2) Mouth inferior.

(3) Lower lip with knob of skin.

(4) Lateral line scales: 33–37.

(5) Subopercle triangular in shape.

DIMENSIONS: Up to 25 in
(635 mm) and 6 lbs (2.7 kg).

FIN COUNTS: Anal soft fin rays
7–8; dorsal soft fin rays 23–30; pectoral soft fin rays 14–17; pelvic soft fin
rays 8–10.

COLORATION: Dorsal region dull
gray or brown; lateral region silvery
with golden tint; ventral region
white.

COMMENTS: The subopercle of
river carpsuckers is triangular in
shape compared to the rounded subopercle of smallmouth buffalo.

Blue sucker, *Cycleptus elongatus*, 4 in (102 mm)

Blue Sucker

Cycleptus elongatus (Lesueur, 1817)

RANGE: Found in limited numbers in major rivers of the state.

HABITAT: Main channels, deep chutes, and riffles of rivers.

CHARACTERISTICS:

(1) Head small.

(2) Eyes small, closer to posterior margin of opercle than tip of snout.

(3) Mouth small and inferior, over-hung by snout; lips covered with bumps.

(4) Dorsal fin long and falcate; dorsal fin base more than one-third the standard length.

(5) Pectoral fins large and falcate.

(6) Body slender; body depth 4 to 5 times into standard length.

(7) Lateral line scales: 51–60.

DIMENSIONS: Up to 40 in (1016 mm).

FIN COUNTS: Anal soft fin rays 8; dorsal soft fin rays 28–37; pectoral soft fin rays 16–17.

COLORATION: Dorsal and lateral region dark olive or blue-black; ventral region white. Fins are dusky to black. Breeding males are darker and covered with turbercles. Lower lobe of caudal fin of juvenile is black.

COMMENTS: The state considers this species to be threatened.

Creek chubsucker, *Erimyzon oblongus,* 6.2 in (157 mm)

Creek Chubsucker

Erimyzon oblongus (Mitchill, 1814)

RANGE: San Jacinto River basin northward to the Red River. Historical records report the species being found in the Devils River.

HABITAT: Headwaters, rivers, and creeks with pools; might be found in lakes.

CHARACTERISTICS:

(1) Mouth subterminal.

(2) Lips with ridges.

(3) Dorsal region with 5–8 dark blotches, which may be absent.

(4) Lateral line absent; 39–45 lateral series scales.

(5) Lateral region with 5–8 dark blotches, which may appear as vertical bars on juveniles, as a lateral stripe on adults, or may be absent.

DIMENSIONS: Up to 16.5 in (419 mm).

FIN COUNTS: Anal soft fin rays 7; dorsal soft fin rays 10–12; pectoral soft fin rays 13–16; pelvic soft fin rays 8–10.

COLORATION: Scales of dorsal and upper lateral region edged with melanophores. Dorsal region blue-green to brown; lateral region yellow or gold; ventral region yellow to white. Paired and median fins yellow-orange to gray. Juveniles have a dark lateral stripe with a yellow stripe above it running from the tip of the snout to the caudal fin base. Breeding males are dark brown on the dorsal and lateral regions with the ventral region pink-yellow.

COMMENTS: This species is listed by the state as threatened.

Lake chubsucker, *Erimyzon sucetta*, 3.4 in (86 mm)

Lake Chubsucker
Erimyzon sucetta (Lacépède, 1803)

RANGE: Brazos River basin northward to the Red River. A disjunct population has been found in the upper reaches of the Guadalupe River.

HABITAT: Lakes, swamps, ponds, sloughs. Might occur in creeks (rare).

CHARACTERISTICS:

(1) Snout rounded.

(2) Mouth subterminal.

(3) Pigmentation forms midlateral stripe from tip of snout to caudal fin base; most notable on juveniles.

(4) Lateral line absent; 34–38 lateral series scales.

(5) Anal fin bilobed on breeding males.

DIMENSIONS: Up to 16 in (406 mm).

FIN COUNTS: Anal soft fin rays 7; dorsal soft fin rays 10–12; pectoral soft fin rays 14–16; pelvic soft fin rays 8–10.

COLORATION: Dorsal region olive-brown; lateral region light olive with pigmentation forming a midlateral stripe from tip of snout to caudal fin base that is most notable in juveniles; ventral region white.

Smallmouth buffalo, *Ictiobus bubalus,* 10 in (254 mm)

Smallmouth Buffalo

Ictiobus bubalus (Rafinesque, 1818)

RANGE: Statewide, excluding the Panhandle.

HABITAT: Lakes, reservoirs and river channels, pools and backwaters.

CHARACTERISTICS:

(1) Snout pointed; overhangs mouth.

(2) Mouth subterminal.

(3) Anterior edge of upper lip far below lower edge of eye.

(4) Deep grooves on thick upper lip.

(5) Nape strongly keeled; most notable on adults.

(6) Lateral line scales: 36–42.

DIMENSIONS: Up to 48 in (1219 mm) and 97 lbs (44 kg).

FIN COUNTS: Anal fin rays 9; dorsal fin rays 26–31; pectoral fin rays 10; pelvic fin rays 9–11.

COLORATION: Dorsal region green or bronze with shade of blue; lateral region olive-yellow to black; ventral region pale yellow to white. The fins can be black or olive. Specimens taken from turbid water will have light colors.

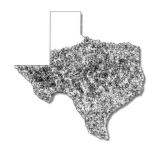

Spotted sucker, *Minytrema melanops*, 9.4 in (239 mm)

Spotted Sucker

Minytrema melanops (Rafinesque, 1820)

RANGE: Brazos River basin northeastward to the Red River. There is also a disjunct population in the Llano River (Colorado River basin).

HABITAT: Impoundments as well as rivers and creeks in pools.

CHARACTERISTICS:

(1) Mouth inferior.

(2) Dorsal and lateral scale bases have spots that form 8–12 horizontal rows along body; may be absent on juveniles.

(3) Posterior edge of dorsal fin darkly pigmented; most notable on juveniles.

(4) Lateral line incomplete or interrupted and absent on juveniles; 42–47 lateral series scales.

(5) Tip of lower lobe of caudal fin darkly pigmented.

DIMENSIONS: Up to 18 in (457 mm) and 2 lbs (0.9 kg).

FIN COUNTS: Anal soft fin rays 7; dorsal soft fin rays 11–13; pectoral soft fin rays 16–18; pelvic soft fin rays 9–10.

COLORATION: Dorsal region dark green or olive-brown; lateral region yellow to brown; ventral region gray to white. Median fins are light yellow-orange to slate-olive; paired fins white. Juveniles have pink median fins. The posterior edges of the dorsal fin and the lower lobe of the caudal fin are darkly pigmented. Dorsal and lateral scale bases with spots form 8–12 horizontal rows along body. Breeding males have two dark midlateral stripes.

Gray redhorse, *Moxostoma congestum,* 10 in (254 mm)

Gray Redhorse

Moxostoma congestum (Baird and Girard, 1854)

RANGE: Rio Grande, Brazos, Colorado, Guadalupe, San Antonio, Nueces, and Pecos river drainages.

HABITAT: Lakes and rivers in pools and runs.

CHARACTERISTICS:

(1) Thick lips with striations and bumps in corners of mouth.

(2) Lower lip with long median groove.

(3) Lateral line scales: 42–46.

(4) Pectoral fin length equal to head length.

DIMENSIONS: Up to 25.5 in (65 mm).

FIN COUNTS: Dorsal soft fin rays 11–12; pectoral soft fin rays 16–17.

COLORATION: Dorsal and lateral regions olive to yellow-gray; ventral region white to pale yellow. The dorsal and caudal fins are gray with anal and paired fins yellow. Breeding males are brassy with orange to yellow fins.

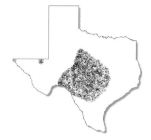

Golden redhorse, *Moxostoma erythrurum,* 4 in (101 mm)

Golden Redhorse

Moxostoma erythrurum (Rafinesque, 1818)

RANGE: Red River basin.

HABITAT: Usually found in lakes and rivers with pools, runs, and riffles.

CHARACTERISTICS:

(1) Lips striated.

(2) Lower lip forms U or V shape on posterior edge.

(3) Dorsal and upper lateral scale edges with pigment.

(4) Lateral line scales: 37–45.

DIMENSIONS: Up to 24 in (610 mm).

FIN COUNTS: Anal soft fin rays 7; dorsal soft fin rays 12–14; pectoral soft fin rays 16–19; pelvic soft fin rays 9.

COLORATION: Dorsal region olive; lateral region brown, with dorsal and upper lateral scale edges pigmented; ventral region white. Juveniles possess three saddle bands on the dorsal region, and breeding males have two midlateral bands.

Blacktail red-
horse, *Moxos-
toma poecilurum*,
6.6 in (168 mm)

Blacktail Redhorse

Moxostoma poecilurum Jordan, 1877

RANGE: San Jacinto River basin
eastward to the Sabine River basin.
HABITAT: Impoundments and rivers in pools and runs.
CHARACTERISTICS:
(1) Melanophores at bases of dorsal
    and lateral scales form horizontal
    stripes.
(2) Lateral line scales: 41–44.
(3) Lower lobe of caudal fin with
    black streak; ventral edge of caudal
    fin is white.
DIMENSIONS: Up to 20 in
(508 mm).
FIN COUNTS: Anal soft fin rays 7;
dorsal soft fin rays 11–13; pectoral
soft fin rays 15–18; pelvic soft fin
rays 8–9.

COLORATION: Dorsal and lateral
regions olive with melanophores
at scale bases forming horizontal
stripes; ventral region white. Lower
lobe of caudal fin with black streak;
ventral margin of caudal fin edge
white.

Mexican tetra, *Astyanax mexicanus*, 2.5 in (64 mm)

Mexican Tetra
Astyanax mexicanus (De Filippi, 1853)

RANGE: May be found statewide due to bait bucket releases; most successful introductions occur in areas with spring flows.

HABITAT: Springs, creeks, and rivers in pools and backwaters.

CHARACTERISTICS:

(1) Snout blunt.

(2) Mouth terminal; jaws with sharp, pointed incisors.

(3) Deep, laterally compressed body.

(4) Black midlateral stripe on caudal peduncle that runs through caudal fin.

(5) Adipose fin present.

DIMENSIONS: Up to 4.8 in (122 mm).

FIN COUNTS: Anal soft fin rays 21–23; dorsal soft fin rays 10–11.

COLORATION: Dorsal region dark olive; lateral region silver with black midlateral stripe on caudal peduncle running through the caudal fin. Fins on large specimens are yellow with red on caudal and anal fins.

Black bullhead,
Ameiurus melas,
4.6 in (117 mm)

Black Bullhead

Ameiurus melas (Rafinesque, 1820)

RANGE: Statewide, excluding the Trans-Pecos area.

HABITAT: Impoundments, oxbows, ponds, creeks, and rivers in pools and backwaters.

CHARACTERISTICS:
(1) Black chin barbels.
(2) Mouth terminal.
(3) Posterior edge of pectoral spines with small serrations.
(4) Adipose fin free.
(5) Caudal fin slightly emarginate.
(6) Anal fin slightly rounded.

DIMENSIONS: Usually 16 in (406 mm) and less than 1 lb (0.5 kg).

FIN COUNTS: Anal soft fin rays 15–21; dorsal fin soft rays 5–6; pectoral soft fin soft rays 9; pelvic soft fin rays 8.

COLORATION: Dorsal and lateral region black to brownish yellow; ventral region yellow to white. Black bullhead fin rays are light colored with fin membranes dark. Juveniles are black.

COMMENTS: It is estimated that the black bullhead has 100,000 taste buds on its body, allowing it to detect potential food items.

Yellow bullhead,
Ameiurus natalis,
8 in (203 mm)

Yellow Bullhead

Ameiurus natalis (Lesueur, 1819)

RANGE: Statewide, excluding the western portions of the Panhandle and South Plains, and the Trans-Pecos.

HABITAT: Impoundments, oxbows, and ponds, as well as rivers and creeks in pools and backwaters.

CHARACTERISTICS:

(1) Yellow or white chin barbels.

(2) Mouth terminal.

(3) Posterior edge of pectoral spines with 5–8 well developed serrations; serrations blunt on older specimens.

(4) Adipose fin free.

(5) Anal fin with a slightly straight edge.

(6) Caudal fin slightly emarginate.

DIMENSIONS: Up to 12 in (305 mm) and 2 lbs (0.9 kg).

FIN COUNTS: Anal soft fin rays 24–28; dorsal soft fin rays 6; pectoral soft fin rays 9; pelvic soft fin rays 8.

COLORATION: Dorsal region olive, yellow, or black; lateral region a light shade of olive, yellow, or black; ventral region pale yellow or white. Yellow bullhead fins are dark with black margins. Juveniles are black.

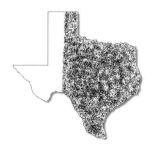

Blue catfish, *Ictalurus furcatus,* adult, 10 in (254 mm)

Blue catfish, *Ictalurus furcatus,* juvenile 3 in (76 mm)

Blue Catfish

Ictalurus furcatus (Lesueur, 1840)

RANGE: Statewide, excluding portions of northwest Texas.

HABITAT: Deep water of impoundments and rivers in backwaters.

CHARACTERISTICS:

(1) Body hump anterior to dorsal fin; most notable on adults.

(2) Posterior edge of pectoral spines with well-developed serrations.

(3) Adipose fin free.

(4) Anal fin with straight edge.

(5) Caudal fin deeply forked.

DIMENSIONS: Up to 5 ft (1524 mm) and 130 lbs (59 kg).

FIN COUNTS: Anal soft fin rays 30–36; dorsal soft fin rays 6–7; pelvic soft fin rays 8.

COLORATION: Dorsal region bluish to gray; lateral region bluish to gray; ventral region white. Fins are light colored with dark margins.

COMMENTS: There is a race of blue catfish (or a distinct new species) occurring in the Rio Grande that has black spots covering its body.

Headwater catfish, *Ictalurus lupus,* 12.4 in (315 mm)

Headwater Catfish
Ictalurus lupus (Girard, 1858)

RANGE: Pecos River and Rio Grande drainages. This catfish was once widespread throughout Central Texas but is now thought to be extirpated from that area.

HABITAT: Spring-fed rivers and creeks in riffles, runs, and pools.

CHARACTERISTICS:
(1) Broad snout and head.
(2) Mouth broad and terminal.
(3) Mouth barbels present.
(4) Lateral region with numerous black spots; may not be as numerous or notable on juveniles.
(5) Adipose fin free.
(6) Forked caudal fin.
(7) Anal fin rounded.

DIMENSIONS: Up to 19 in (483 mm).

FIN COUNTS: Anal soft fin rays 22–26.

COLORATION: Dorsal region black to blue; lateral region pale blue to olive with numerous black spots; ventral region white. Mouth barbels are white to dusky.

COMMENTS: The headwater catfish can be distinguished from the channel catfish by its 22–26 anal fin rays versus 27–29 anal fin rays for the channel catfish. Identification can be verified by the use of canonical scores such as those used by Kelsch and Hendricks (1990).

Channel catfish, *Ictalurus punctatus,* adult, 12 in (305 mm)

Channel catfish, *Ictalurus punctatus,* juvenile, 2.8 in (71.2 mm)

Channel Catfish

Ictalurus punctatus (Rafinesque, 1818)

RANGE: Statewide.

HABITAT: Lakes and rivers in pools and runs.

CHARACTERISTICS:

(1) Upper jaw slightly overhangs lower jaw.

(2) Spots on dorsal and lateral region; may be absent on juveniles or large adults.

(3) Posterior edge of pectoral spines with well-developed serrations.

(4) Lateral region with black spots; may be absent on large adults.

(5) Adipose fin free.

(6) Anal fin rounded.

(7) Caudal fin forked.

DIMENSIONS: Up to 44 in and 41 lbs (18.6 kg).

FIN COUNTS: Anal soft fin rays 24–29; dorsal soft fin rays 6–7; pelvic soft fin rays 8.

COLORATION: Dorsal region pale blue to olive; lateral region pale blue to olive with black spots; ventral region white. Dorsal and lateral regions with spots, which may be absent on juveniles or large specimens. Median fins have dark margins.

COMMENTS: The channel catfish has been introduced into many creeks and reservoirs. See comments on the headwater catfish.

Tadpole madtom, *Noturus gyrinus,* 3.7 in (94 mm)

Tadpole Madtom
Noturus gyrinus (Mitchill, 1817)

RANGE: Nueces River basin northward to the Red River basin.

HABITAT: Rivers and creeks in pools and backwaters having undercut banks with exposed tree roots.

CHARACTERISTICS:

(1) Mouth terminal, with jaws equal; upper or lower jaw do not notably extend past each other.

(2) Posterior edges of pectoral spines lack serrations.

(3) Thin, black midlateral stripe from head to caudal fin base. Muscle segments visible due to thin lines running off of midlateral stripe.

(4) Adipose fin continuous with caudal fin.

(5) Caudal fin rounded; may be pointed in some individuals.

DIMENSIONS: Up to 5 in (127 mm).

FIN COUNTS: Anal soft fin rays 13–18; pectoral soft fin rays 5–10; pelvic soft fin rays 5.

COLORATION: Dorsal light tan to brown; lateral region light tan to brown with thin, dark midlateral stripe; ventral region white or pale yellow. Fins are light tan to brown. Adults may have orange on lower jaw and throat.

COMMENTS: The tadpole madtom can be distinguished the from freckled madtom by the upper and lower jaws being equal to each other and by its having a thin, dark midlateral stripe.

Freckled madtom, *Noturus nocturnus,* 2.4 in (61 mm)

Freckled Madtom

Noturus nocturnus Jordan and
Gilbert, 1886

RANGE: Brazos River basin northward to the Red River.
HABITAT: Rivers and creeks in
riffles and undercut banks with
exposed tree roots.
CHARACTERISTICS:
(1) Upper jaw protrudes over lower
    jaw.
(2) Posterior edge of pectoral spines
    with 3–4 faint serrations.
(3) Adipose fin continuous with cau-
    dal fin.
(4) Caudal fin rounded.
DIMENSIONS: Up to 5.8 in
(147 mm).

FIN COUNTS: Anal soft fin rays
16–18; pectoral soft fin rays 7–14;
pelvic soft fin rays 9.
COLORATION: Dorsal and lateral
regions brownish gray; ventral region
white to pale yellow with melanophores. Fins are dark gray with caudal fin having a thin white margin.
COMMENTS: See comments on the
tadpole madtom.

Flathead catfish, *Pylodictis olivaris*, 9.9 in (251 mm)

Flathead Catfish

Pylodictis olivaris (Rafinesque, 1818)

RANGE: Statewide.

HABITAT: Lakes, impoundments, and rivers and creeks in pools.

CHARACTERISTICS:

(1) Head depressed dorsally.

(2) Lower jaw extends beyond upper jaw, except in juveniles.

(3) Band of premaxillary teeth with backward extensions.

(4) Anterior and posterior edges of pectoral spines with serrations.

(5) Adipose fin free.

(6) Caudal fin slightly emarginate.

(7) Upper lobe of caudal fin with white tip; may not be notable on large adults.

DIMENSIONS: Up to 61 in (1549 mm).

FIN COUNTS: Anal soft fin rays 12–17; dorsal soft fin rays 6; pectoral soft fin rays 11; pelvic soft fin rays 9.

COLORATION: Dorsal and lateral region with a mottled pattern of yellow and brown. Specimens taken from clear water have a dark brown dorsal region as opposed to a yellow dorsal region for those taken from turbid water. Ventral region white to pale yellow. Fins with coloration similar to dorsal and lateral regions. Upper lobe of caudal fin has a white tip, which may not be present on large adults. Large flatheads are usually yellow-brown with a faded mottling pattern.

COMMENTS: Adults feed primarily on live fish as opposed to other catfish species, which feed on semiaquatic insect larvae, crustaceans, algae, mollusks, and fish.

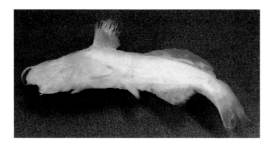

Toothless blindcat, *Trogloglanis pattersoni,* 3.4 in (86 mm)

Toothless Blindcat

Trogloglanis pattersoni Eigenmann, 1919

RANGE: San Antonio Pool of the Edwards Aquifer (near San Antonio) at depths of 976–1862 ft (300–600 m).
HABITAT: Subterranean water.
CHARACTERISTICS:
(1) No eyes.
(2) Jaws without teeth.
(3) Lips thin at corners of mouth.
(4) Head and snout rounded; snout hangs over mouth.
(5) Lower jaw curved upward into mouth.
(6) Entire body white or pink due to blood pigmentation.
(7) Adipose fin joined to caudal fin.
DIMENSIONS: Up to 4 in (102 mm).

FIN COUNTS: Anal soft fin rays 16–17.
COLORATION: Entire body white or pink (due to blood pigmentation). Considered threatened due to pumping of the Edwards Aquifer as well as potential pollutants from surface water runoff.
COMMENTS: This species is listed by the state as threatened.

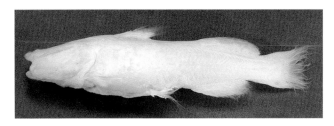

Widemouth blindcat, *Satan eurystomus*, 4 in (102 mm)

Widemouth Blindcat

Satan eurystomus Hubbs and Bailey, 1947

RANGE: San Antonio Pool of the Edwards Aquifer (near San Antonio) at depths of 976–1862 ft (300–600 m).
HABITAT: Subterranean water.
CHARACTERISTICS:
(1) No eyes.
(2) Teeth in jaws well developed.
(3) Head broad and depressed dorsally.
(4) Snout long.
(5) Gill membranes separate with fold between membranes.
(6) Lips thick at corner of mouth.
(7) Entire body white or pink due to blood pigments.
(8) Adipose fin free.
DIMENSIONS: Up to 5.3 in (135 mm).
FIN COUNTS: Anal soft fin rays 19–20.
COLORATION: Entire body white or pink (due to blood pigmentation).
COMMENTS: This species is listed by the state as threatened due to pumping of the Edwards Aquifer as well as potential pollutants from surface water runoff.

Suckermouth catfish, *Hypostomus plecostomus,* 4.5 in (114 mm)

Suckermouth Catfish

Hypostomus plecostomus (Linnaeus, 1758)

RANGE: Currently found in portions of Central and South Texas, but may be found statewide as the result of aquarium releases.

HABITAT: Rivers in pools and runs.

CHARACTERISTICS:

(1) Suckerlike mouth.

(2) Dorsal and lateral regions with rows of bony plates.

(3) Dorsal, pectoral, and pelvic fins with a spine.

(4) Body and fins with black and brown stripes or spots.

DIMENSIONS: Up to 18 in (457 mm).

FIN COUNTS: Dorsal soft fin rays 7.

COLORATION: Body and fins with black and brown stripes or spots.

Redfin pickerel,
Esox americanus,
9.1 in (231 mm)

Redfin Pickerel

Esox americanus (Lesueur, 1789)

RANGE: Brazos River basin northeastward to the Red River basin.

HABITAT: Lakes and swamps as well as rivers and creeks in pools and backwaters.

CHARACTERISTICS:

(1) Cheeks and opercles fully scaled.

(2) Slanted, dark suborbital bars.

(3) Jaws large with canine teeth.

(4) Branchiostegal rays: 11–13.

(5) Snout short; distance from tip of snout to center of eye equal to or less than distance from center of eye to rear margin of operculum.

(6) Pale areas on greenish to bronze lateral region give impression of wavy vertical bars, which are most notable in adults; a faint midlateral stripe may be notable.

(7) Lateral line weakly developed; 92–118 scales.

DIMENSIONS: Up to 15 in (381 mm) and 0.75 lbs (0.34 kg).

FIN COUNTS: Anal soft fin rays 13–15; dorsal soft fin rays 14–17; pectoral soft fin rays 14–15; pelvic soft fin rays 10–11.

COLORATION: Dorsal region greenish to bronze; lateral region greenish to bronze with pale areas forming wavy vertical bars; ventral region white to amber. Head with dark, slanted suborbital bars and fins with a yellow or red coloration.

Chain pickerel,
Esox niger, 9.5 in
(240 mm)

Chain Pickerel
Esox niger Lesueur, 1818

RANGE: Red and Sabine river drainages.

HABITAT: Lakes, swamps, and backwaters, as well as creeks and rivers with pools.

CHARACTERISTICS:

(1) Cheek and opercle fully scaled.

(2) Snout long; distance from tip of snout to center of eye greater than distance from center of eye to rear margin of operculum.

(3) Dark, vertical suborbital bar.

(4) Jaws large with notable canine teeth.

(5) Branchiostegal rays: 14–17.

(6) Chainlike pattern on lateral region of body, which is most notable in adults; wavy bars on juveniles.

(7) Lateral line poorly developed; 110–38 scales.

DIMENSIONS: Up to 9.1 lbs (4.1 kg).

FIN COUNTS: Anal soft fin rays 13; dorsal soft fin rays 14.

COLORATION: Head with a dark, vertical suborbital bar. Dorsal region olive-yellow or olive; lateral region light green-yellow with dark chainlike markings, most notably on adults. Juveniles (under 8 in) have barring similar to that of the redfin pickerel.

COMMENTS: The chain pickerel may be distinguished from the redfin pickerel by its dark, vertical suborbital bar, long snout, and 14–17 branchiostegal rays.

Rainbow trout, *Oncorhynchus mykiss*, 11 in (279 mm)

Rainbow Trout

Oncorhynchus mykiss (Walbaum, 1792)

RANGE: May be found statewide as a result of seasonal stocking from hatcheries of the Texas Parks and Wildlife Department. The only reproducing rainbow trout population is found in McKittrick Canyon in the Guadalupe Mountains

HABITAT: Cold water of lakes, headwaters, creeks, and rivers.

CHARACTERISTICS:

(1) Mouth terminal; teeth on jaws, palatine bones, and tip of tongue.
(2) Upper jaw reaches just past posterior margin of eye.
(3) Black spots on head, dorsal, and lateral regions, and median fins.
(4) Lateral line scales: 100–50.
(5) Adipose fin with dark margin; most notable on juveniles.

DIMENSIONS: Up to 19 lbs (8.6 kg).

FIN COUNTS: Anal soft fin rays 8–12; dorsal soft fin rays 10–12; pelvic soft fin rays 11–17; pelvic soft fin rays 9–10.

COLORATION: Dorsal region yellow-green to brown; lateral and ventral regions silver to pale yellow-green. Stream-based and breeding rainbow trout have darker colors.

Pirate perch, *Aphredoderus sayanus,* 3.4 in (86 mm)

Pirate Perch

Aphredoderus sayanus (Gilliams, 1824)

RANGE: Lower Brazos River basin northward to the Red River basin.

HABITAT: Swamps, sloughs, ponds, and lakes, as well as rivers and creeks in pools and backwaters.

CHARACTERISTICS:

(1) Head large; dark, suborbital bars present.

(2) Mouth large and terminal.

(3) Lateral line incomplete or absent; 48–59 lateral series scales.

(4) Dorsal fin with 2–3 weak spines.

(5) Pectoral fins with 1 weak spine.

(6) Anal fin with 2–3 weak spines.

(7) Anus and urogenital pore positioned just behind isthmus.

(8) Caudal fin slightly emarginate.

DIMENSIONS: Up to 5.5 in (140 mm).

FIN COUNTS: Anal soft fin rays 6; dorsal soft fin rays 9–10; pectoral soft fin rays 12–13; pelvic soft fin rays 7.

COLORATION: Head with dark, vertical suborbital bars. Dorsal region olive to black; lateral region light shade of olive to black with flecks of iridescent blue, copper-green, or silver; ventral region pale yellow. Breeding males have black on head with dorsal region a shade of violet.

COMMENTS: As a pirate perch matures, the position of the anus and urogenital pore moves forward until it is situated just behind the isthmus. Studies have found that such a position for the urogenital pore allows for incubation of eggs in the gill chamber; it has been observed that after the eggs have been laid they travel along a groove into the gill chamber. Researchers believe that the eggs in the gill chamber are a prelude to buccal incubation of eggs.

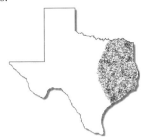

Mountain mullet, *Agonostomus monticola,* 2.5 in (64 mm)

Mountain Mullet

Agonostomus monticola (Bancroft, 1834)

RANGE: Trinity River basin westward to the Rio Grande basin.

HABITAT: Bays and estuaries, but may be found considerable distances inland in rivers.

CHARACTERISTICS:

(1) Adipose eyelids absent.

(2) Mouth small and terminal.

(3) Ctenoid scales.

(4) Large blue spot at base of pectoral fins; may be absent.

(5) Anal fin with 2 spines.

DIMENSIONS: Up to 30 in (762 mm).

FIN COUNTS: Anal soft fin rays 8; dorsal soft fin rays 8.

COLORATION: Dorsal region blue or green; lateral region silvery; ventral region white. Large blue spot at base of pectoral fins.

Striped mullet,
Mugil cephalus,
8 in (203 mm)

Striped Mullet
Mugil cephalus Linnaeus, 1758

RANGE: Along the Gulf Coast and in rivers as far inland as Lake Texoma and the Colorado River near Austin.

HABITAT: Bays and estuaries, but may be found considerable distances inland in rivers.

CHARACTERISTICS:

(1) Adipose eyelids.

(2) Mouth small and terminal.

(3) Scales cycloid.

(4) Dorsal and lateral regions with dark, horizontal stripes; stripes may not be notable on juveniles under 6 in.

(5) Large blue spot at base of pectoral fins.

(6) First dorsal fin with 4 spines; second dorsal fin with 1 spine.

(7) Anal fin with 3 spines; third spine on juveniles not yet developed and is a soft ray.

(8) Soft ray portions of dorsal and anal fins with a few scales.

(9) Lateral line absent; 38–42 lateral series scales.

DIMENSIONS: Up to 30 in (762 mm).

FIN COUNTS: Anal soft fin rays 8; dorsal soft fin rays 8.

COLORATION: Dorsal region blue; lateral region silvery; ventral region white. Dorsal and lateral region with dark, horizontal stripes and large blue spot at base of each pectoral fin.

Brook silverside, *Labidesthes sicculus,* 4.6 in (117 mm)

Brook Silverside

Labidesthes sicculus (Cope, 1865)

RANGE: Brazos River basin north and east to portions of the Red and Sabine river basins.

HABITAT: Open surface water of lakes, ponds, rivers, and creeks in pools.

CHARACTERISTICS:

(1) Snout long and beaklike.

(2) Head long and flattened dorsally.

(3) Dorsal and upper lateral region scales lightly pigmented.

(4) Silver midlateral stripe.

(5) First dorsal fin, 4–5 flexible spines; second dorsal fin, 1 flexible spine.

(6) Anal fin, 1 flexible spine.

(7) Pelvic fins, 1 flexible spine.

(8) Lateral line absent; 74–87 lateral series scales.

(9) Caudal fin forked.

DIMENSIONS: Up to 5 in (127 mm).

FIN COUNTS: Anal soft fin rays 21–27; dorsal soft fin rays 10–11; pectoral soft fin rays 12–15; pelvic soft fin rays 5.

COLORATION: Dorsal region pale green; lateral region silvery with silver midlateral stripe; ventral region silver-white. The scale edges of the dorsal and upper lateral regions are outlined with melanophores.

COMMENTS: The brook silverside can be distinguished from the inland silverside and rough silverside by its smaller scales, larger lateral series count (74–87 versus 34–48 scales for the inland silverside and rough silverside), a pointed snout as compared to a more rounded snout on the inland silverside and rough silverside, and smooth scales versus the rough scales (ctenoid scales) on the rough silverside.

Inland silverside,
Menidia beryllina,
5.3 in (135 mm)

Inland Silverside

Menidia beryllina (Cope, 1867)

RANGE: Statewide.
HABITAT: Coastal rivers, creeks, and reservoirs as a result of introductions.
CHARACTERISTICS:
(1) Snout short and rounded.
(2) Head long and flat dorsally.
(3) Scales of dorsal and upper lateral region outlined with melanophores.
(4) Silver midlateral stripe.
(5) First dorsal fin, 4–5 flexible spines; second dorsal fin, 1 flexible spine.
(6) Pelvic fins, 1 flexible spine.
(7) Anal fin, 1 flexible spine.
(8) Lateral line absent; 34–44 lateral series scales.
(9) Caudal fin forked.
DIMENSIONS: Up to 6 in (152 mm).
FIN COUNTS: Anal soft fin rays 14–21; dorsal soft fin rays 8–9; pectoral soft fin rays 13–15; pelvic soft fin rays 5.

COLORATION: Dorsal region pale green; lateral region with silver midlateral stripe; ventral region silvery white. Melanophores on scale edges of dorsal and upper lateral regions.
COMMENTS: See comments for brook silverside. The inland silverside can be distinguished from the rough silverside by its smooth, cycloid versus rough scales; the ctenoid scales of the rough silverside, with dorsal and upper lateral region scale edges darkly pigmented as opposed to the rough silverside's having only light scale pigmentation on dorsal and upper lateral regions and four rows of dark spots on the dorsal region; and lack of scales covering the bases of the dorsal and anal fins as opposed to scales covering the bases of dorsal and anal fins of the rough silverside.

Rough silverside, *Membras martinica,*
3.3 in (84 mm)

Rough Silverside

Membras martinica (Valenciennes, 1835)

RANGE: Coastal areas as well as Amistad, Falcon, and Canyon Lake reservoirs due to introductions.
HABITAT: Deep, saline portions of bays and coastal waters.
CHARACTERISTICS:
(1) Snout short and rounded.
(2) Dorsal region with 4 rows black spots.
(3) Dorsal fin base covered with scales.
(4) Silver midlateral stripe.
(5) Scales rough due to ctenoid scales; roughness may not be easily notable.
(6) First dorsal fin, 5 flexible spines; second dorsal fin, 1 flexible spine.
(7) Anal fin, 1 flexible spine.
(8) Lateral line absent; 43–48 lateral series scales.
(9) Anal fin base covered with scales.
(10) Posterior margin of caudal fin dark; may not be notable.
DIMENSIONS: Up to 3.5 in (89 mm).
FIN COUNTS: Anal soft fin rays 14–21; dorsal soft fin rays 7.
COLORATION: Dorsal region pale green with four rows of black spots; lateral region silvery with bright silver midlateral stripe; ventral region silvery white.
COMMENTS: See comments for inland silverside and brook silverside.

Western mosquitofish,
Gambusia affinis, female,
1.7 in (43 mm)

Western Mosquitofish

Gambusia affinis (Baird and Girard, 1853)

RANGE: Statewide.

HABITAT: Ponds, lakes, and creeks in pools and backwaters.

CHARACTERISTICS:

(1) Mouth superior.

(2) Dark suborbital bars.

(3) Dorsal and lateral scales outlined with melanophores.

(4) Dark middorsal stripe anterior to dorsal fin base.

(5) Black specks on dorsal and lateral region; may be absent.

(6) Thin, black midlateral stripe.

(7) Lateral line absent; 29–32 lateral series scales.

(8) Dorsal and caudal fins with 1–3 rows of black spots.

(9) First few rays of anal fin elongate, males only (gonopodium).

(10) Large, dark spot near anus, pregnant females only.

DIMENSIONS: Up to 2.5 in (64 mm).

FIN COUNTS: Anal soft fin rays 7; dorsal soft fin rays 6–7 (rarely 7); pectoral fin soft rays 12–14; pelvic soft fin rays 6.

COLORATION: Head with dark suborbital bars. Dorsal region olive with middorsal stripe anterior to dorsal fin base and a few scattered small, black specks; lateral region silvery with thin, black midlateral line and scattered small, black specks; ventral region silvery. Dorsal and anal fins of mosquitofish have 1–3 rows of black spots. Dorsal and lateral scales outlined with melanophores.

Big Bend gam-
busia, *Gambusia
gaigei*, male,
1.8 in (46 mm)

Big Bend gam-
busia, *Gambusia
gaigei*, female,
1.5 in (38 mm)

Big Bend Gambusia

Gambusia gaigei Hubbs, 1929

RANGE: Springs east of Rio Grande Village and Boquillas Crossing in Big Bend National Park.

HABITAT: Spring headwaters.

CHARACTERISTICS:

(1) Dark suborbital bars may be absent.

(2) Dorsal and upper lateral scales with melanophores forming crescent-shaped markings.

(3) Dark middorsal stripe; may be absent.

(4) Row of dark spots on lower third of dorsal fin; outer margin dark.

(5) Dark midlateral stripe.

(6) First few rays of anal fin elongate, males only (gonopodium).

(7) Large, dark spot near anus, females only.

DIMENSIONS: Up to 2.3 in (58 mm).

FIN COUNTS: Dorsal soft fin rays 8.

COLORATION: Head with dark suborbital bars. Dorsal region and lateral regions golden olive with melanophores forming crescent-shaped markings on scales; dark middorsal stripe; lateral region silvery with dark midlateral stripe; ventral region white. Large black spot near anus only on females. Row of dark spots on lower third of dorsal fin, with outer margin dark.

COMMENTS: This species is listed by the state as endangered.

Largespring gambusia, *Gambusia geiseri,* 1.2 in (30 mm)

Largespring Gambusia

Gambusia geiseri (Hubbs and Hubbs, 1957)

RANGE: Headwaters of the San Marcos and Comal Rivers; introductions have placed it in the headwaters of the Concho River, San Solomon Springs, Leon Springs, and Independence Creek.

HABITAT: Springs and rivers.

CHARACTERISTICS:

(1) Thin stripe of melanophores across lower lip.

(2) Dark middorsal stripe anterior to dorsal fin base.

(3) Scattered black specks on dorsal and lateral region.

(4) Scale edges outlined with melanophores.

(5) Dorsal and caudal fin with row of black spots, absent on juveniles; additional spots may form faint rows.

(6) Thin, black midlateral stripe.

(7) First few rays of anal fin elongate, males only (gonopodium).

(8) Anal fin with median row of spots, females only.

(9) Melanophores forming midventral line on caudal peduncle.

DIMENSIONS: Up to 1.7 in (43 mm).

FIN COUNTS: Dorsal soft fin rays 7–9.

COLORATION: Lower jaw with a stripe of dark pigment. Dorsal region olive with middorsal stripe anterior to dorsal fin base and scattered black specks; lateral region silver with yellow and iridescent blue with thin, black midlateral stripe and scattered black specks. Dorsal and caudal fins with row of black spots absent on juveniles; there may be additional spots forming faint rows. Melanophores form midventral line on caudal peduncle. Anal fin of females has a single row of black spots.

COMMENTS: The largespring gambusia can be distinguished from the western mosquitofish by the stripe of dark pigment on the lower jaw and presence of a midventral stripe (both of which are absent on the western mosquitofish) and by having only 7–9 dorsal fin rays versus 6 (rarely) or 7 dorsal fin rays on the western mosquitofish.

Pecos gambusia,
Gambusia nobilis,
male, 1.4 in
(36 mm)

Pecos gambusia,
Gambusia nobilis,
female, 1.1 in
(28 mm)

Pecos Gambusia

Gambusia nobilis (Baird and Girard, 1853)

RANGE: Headwaters of Phantom Lake Spring (Jeff Davis County); San Solomon, Giffen, and East Sandia Springs (Reeves County); and Leon Creek and Diamond Y Springs (Pecos County).

HABITAT: Springs with vegetation.

CHARACTERISTICS:

(1) Mouth superior.

(2) Dark suborbital bars.

(3) Dark middorsal stripe to dorsal fin base.

(4) Scales edges on dorsal and lateral regions outlined by melanophores.

(5) Deep bodied.

(6) Arched back.

(7) First few rays of anal fin elongate, males only (gonopodium).

(8) Large dark spot near anus, females only.

DIMENSIONS: Up to 2.5 in (64 mm).

FIN COUNTS: Dorsal soft fin rays 8.

COLORATION: Head with dark suborbital bars. Dorsal region olive with dark middorsal stripe; lateral region silver with blue-yellow tones; ventral region white. Dorsal and lateral scale edges with melanophores. Large dark spot near anus (females only).

COMMENTS: This species is listed by the state as endangered.

Amazon molly, *Poecilia formosa*, 2.7 in (69 mm)

Amazon Molly
Poecilia formosa (Girard, 1859)

RANGE: Lower Rio Grande. This species has been introduced into the San Antonio, San Marcos, and lower Nueces Rivers.

HABITAT: Creeks, sloughs, and ditches in backwaters and pools.

CHARACTERISTICS:
(1) Mouth small.
(2) Head small and depressed.
(3) Scales edges outlined by melanophores; may have horizontal rows of black spots.
(4) Lateral line absent.

DIMENSIONS: Up to 3.7 in (94 mm).

FIN COUNTS: Dorsal fin soft rays 10–12.

COLORATION: Dorsal and lateral regions olive with scale edges darkly pigmented; ventral region white to yellow.

COMMENTS: The Amazon molly is a female-only species. Since there are no male Amazon mollies, the females breed with the males of four other species of the genus *Poecilia*. Of those four species, only the sailfin molly is found in Texas. The Amazon molly can be distinguished from the sailfin molly by its dorsal fin base being less than one-half the predorsal length versus the dorsal fin base being more than one-half the predorsal length for the sailfin mollies; the Amazon molly also does not have the distinct scale pigmentation seen on the sailfin molly.

Sailfin molly, *Poecilia latipinna*, male, 3.8 in (97 mm)

Sailfin molly, *Poecilia latipinna*, female, 2.2 in (56 mm)

Sailfin Molly

Poecilia latipinna (Lesueur, 1821)

RANGE: Central Texas headwaters and the lower Rio Grande basin.
HABITAT: Ponds, lakes, sloughs, and creeks in backwaters and pools.
CHARACTERISTICS:
(1) Mouth small and superior.
(2) Head small and depressed dorsally.
(3) Brown spots on scales forming 5–8 horizontal stripes on lateral region.
(4) Lateral region with scales outlined by melanophores; most notable on males.
(5) Large, saillike dorsal fin; smaller on females.
(6) Dorsal portion of dorsal fin with black spots; most notable on males.
(7) Lateral line absent; 23–28 lateral series scales.
(8) Caudal fin with orange spots on large males.
(9) Posterior margin of caudal fin black; may be absent.
DIMENSIONS: Up to 6 in (152 mm).
FIN COUNTS: Dorsal soft fin rays 12–16.
COLORATION: Dorsal region olive with brown spots on scales forming horizontal rows; lateral region olive with brown scale spots or dashes forming horizontal rows; ventral region white or yellow. Dorsal fin with black spots. Large males have an iridescent blue dorsal region with orange on lower head and breast and orange spots on a purple-blue caudal fin.
COMMENTS: See comments on the Amazon molly.

Golden topminnow, *Fundulus chrysotus,* male, 3 in (76 mm)

Golden topminnow, *Fundulus chrysotus,* female, 2.3 in (58 mm)

Golden Topminnow
Fundulus chrysotus (Gunther, 1866)

RANGE: Lavaca River basin northeast to the Sabine River basin.

HABITAT: Swamps and sloughs as well as rivers and creeks in pools and backwaters.

CHARACTERISTICS:

(1) Lateral region with gold spots.

(2) Dark, vertical bars (8–11) on lateral region; absent on juveniles and females.

(3) Lateral line absent; 30–35 lateral series scales.

(4) Median fins with red-brown spots, breeding and large males only.

(5) Posterior portion of lateral region speckled with red-brown dots, breeding males only.

DIMENSIONS: Up to 3 in (76 mm).

FIN COUNTS: Anal soft fin rays 9–11; dorsal soft fin rays 7–9.

COLORATION: Dorsal region yellow-green; lateral region yellow-green with dark, vertical bars and gold spots. Breeding male golden topminnows have red-brown spots on posterior portion of lateral region and median fins. Females and juveniles are olive-green or gray with small, bluish spots. Females can have faint horizontal stripes on lateral region.

Starhead topminnow, *Fundulus dispar,* 2.5 (64 mm)

Starhead Topminnow

Fundulus dispar (Agassiz, 1854)

RANGE: Brazos River basin northward to the Red River basin.

HABITAT: Standing water and creeks in pools and backwaters.

CHARACTERISTICS:

(1) Snout broad and round.

(2) Mouth large.

(3) Dark subopercle bars, may be absent.

(4) Golden spot on top of head.

(5) Red or brown spots forming horizontal stripes on lateral region.

(6) Dark, vertical bars (3–13) on juveniles and males; may be absent.

DIMENSIONS: Up to 3 in (76 mm).

FIN COUNTS: Anal soft fin rays 10–12; dorsal soft fin rays 6–8; pectoral soft fin rays 12–14; pelvic soft fin rays 6.

COLORATION: Head with dark subopercle bar. Dorsal region yellow-green with golden spot on top of head; lateral region silvery with 3–13 dark, vertical bars on juveniles and males; red spots forming lateral stripes on males, with brown spots forming lateral stripes on females. Median fins of males with red spots.

Gulf killifish, *Fundulus grandis,* 5 in (127 mm)

Gulf Killifish

Fundulus grandis Baird and Girard, 1853

RANGE: Brazos, Rio Grande, and Pecos river basins.

HABITAT: Usually found in coastal areas, but also found in freshwater rivers and lakes as a result of migrations from costal habitats and bait bucket introductions.

CHARACTERISTICS:

(1) Lower jaw projects above upper jaw.
(2) Head short, blunt, and wide.
(3) Vertical bars on lateral region of males weakly defined but notable posteriorly.
(4) Yellow spots scattered on body, males only.
(5) Median fins with pale spots, males only.
(6) Nape unscaled to partly scaled.
(7) Pigmentation forms dark blotch on last dorsal fin ray; may be absent.

DIMENSIONS: Up to 6 in (152 mm).

FIN COUNTS: Anal soft fin rays 10–12; dorsal soft fin rays 11.

COLORATION: Males with dark green silvery vertical bars and yellow spots posteriorly; ventral region orange-yellow. Males have a dark blotch on posterior portion of dorsal fin. The median fins have pale spots, and the anterior portion of the pelvic fins are yellow. Females are olive above and light olive below without bars or spots.

Blackstripe top-minnow, *Fundulus notatus,* male, 3.2 in (81 mm)

Blackstripe top-minnow, *Fundulus notatus,* female, 3.1 in (79 mm)

Blackstripe Topminnow
Fundulus notatus (Rafinesque, 1820)

RANGE: San Antonio River basin north and eastward to the Red River basin.

HABITAT: Lakes, ponds, rivers, and creeks.

CHARACTERISTICS:

(1) Mouth terminal.

(2) Scattered dark spots on dorsal and upper lateral region that may be indistinct or absent; spots not as dark as midlateral stripe.

(3) Dark middorsal stripe anterior to dorsal fin base.

(4) Black midlateral stripe from tip of snout onto caudal fin; crossbars on stripe, males only.

(5) Lateral line absent; 29–37 lateral series scales.

(6) Median fins with dark spots; not notable on females.

DIMENSIONS: Up to 3.8 in (97 mm).

FIN COUNTS: Anal soft fin rays 11–13; dorsal soft fin rays 8–12; pectoral soft fin rays 14–15; pelvic soft fin rays 6.

COLORATION: Head with silver-white spot dorsally. Dorsal region has green middorsal stripe anterior to dorsal fin base with scattered dark spots on dorsal and upper lateral region; lateral region has black midlateral stripe from tip of snout onto caudal fin; ventral region white to yellow. Dark spots on median fins.

COMMENTS: The blackstripe topminnow can be distinguished from the blackspotted topminnow in that the dark spots on the dorsal and upper lateral regions are not as dark as the midlateral stripe, whereas the spots on the dorsal and upper lateral regions of the blackspotted topminnow are as dark or darker than the midlateral stripe.

Blackspotted top-
minnow, *Fundulus
olivaceus,* male,
3.3 in (83 mm)

Blackspotted Topminnow
Fundulus olivaceus (Storer, 1845)

RANGE: San Jacinto River basin
north and east to the Red River basin.
HABITAT: Headwaters, rivers, and
creeks.
CHARACTERISTICS:
(1) Dorsal and upper lateral region
with black spots; spots are as dark
or darker than midlateral stripe;
males have more spots as compared
to females.
(2) Dark middorsal stripe anterior to
dorsal fin base, juveniles only; may
be faint.
(3) Dark midlateral stripe from snout
onto caudal fin; adult males have
crossbars on stripe.
(4) Lateral line absent; 32–37 lateral
series scales.
(5) Median fins with dark spots; may
be faint or absent.
DIMENSIONS: Up to 3.7 in
(94 mm).

FIN COUNTS: Anal soft fin rays
10–14; dorsal soft fin rays 8–12; pectoral soft fin rays 13–15; pelvic soft
fin rays 6.
COLORATION: Dorsal and upper
lateral region olive-brown with black
spots and a dark middorsal stripe anterior to dorsal fin base; lateral region
with dark midlateral stripe; ventral
region white. Median fins with dark
spots.
COMMENTS: The blackspotted
topminnow can be distinguished from
the blackstripe topminnow in that
the dark spots on its dorsal and upper
lateral regions are as dark or darker
than the midlateral stripe, whereas
the spots on the dorsal and upper
lateral regions of the blackstripe minnow are not as dark as the midlateral
stripe.

Longnose killifish, *Fundulus similis,* 4.3 in (109 mm)

Longnose Killifish

Fundulus similis (Baird and Girard, 1853)

RANGE: Mainly a marine species that can be found in coastal waters.

HABITAT: Coastal waters and short distances up coastal rivers and creeks.

CHARACTERISTICS:

(1) Snout long.

(2) Faint spot behind opercle on males only; may be absent.

(3) Dark blotch on posterior portion of dorsal fin; most notable on juvenile males.

(4) Dark vertical bars (10–15) on lateral region.

(5) Small, dark spot near dorsal portion of caudal peduncle, may be absent.

DIMENSIONS: Up to 6 in (152 mm).

FIN COUNTS: Anal soft fin rays 10; dorsal soft fin rays 11–14.

COLORATION: Dorsal region olive; lateral region silvery with 10–15 dark, vertical bars and a small black spot near dorsal portion of caudal peduncle. Males have a faint spot behind opercle; juveniles have a dark blotch on the posterior portion of the dorsal fin.

Plains killifish, *Fundulus zebrinus,* male, 3.7 in (94 mm)

Plains killifish, *Fundulus zebrinus,* female, 3.4 in (86 mm)

Plains Killifish

Fundulus zebrinus Jordan and Gilbert, 1883

RANGE: Western portions of the state.

HABITAT: Headwaters, creeks, and rivers in pools, runs, and backwaters.

CHARACTERISTICS:

(1) Mouth terminal.

(2) Dark, vertical bars (12–26) on lateral region; bars wider on males compared to females.

(3) Lateral line absent; 41–68 lateral series scales.

DIMENSIONS: Up to 4 in (102 mm).

FIN COUNTS: Anal soft fin rays 13–14; dorsal soft fin rays 13–16; pelvic soft fin rays 6.

COLORATION: Dorsal region light brown to tan; lateral region with dark barring; ventral region white to yellow. Pectoral fins are yellow. Breeding males have red or bright orange dorsal, anal, and paired fins.

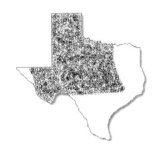

Rainwater killifish, *Lucania parva,*
1.2 in (30 mm)

Rainwater Killifish

Lucania parva (Baird and Girard, 1855)

RANGE: Coastal rivers and creeks, the Rio Grande basin, and portions of the San Saba River basin due to introductions.

HABITAT: Sloughs, ponds, and lakes, as well as rivers and creeks in pools and backwaters.

CHARACTERISTICS:

(1) Mouth small and superior.

(2) Black spot on anterior portion of dorsal fin; absent on females or juveniles.

(3) Fins, except pectorals, with thin black margins.

(4) Dorsal and lateral scales outlined with melanophores.

(5) Body laterally compressed.

(6) Caudal fin slightly rounded.

DIMENSIONS: Up to 2.8 in (71 mm).

FIN COUNTS: Dorsal soft fin rays 9–13.

COLORATION: Dorsal region brown to olive; lateral region silver to yellow; ventral region white. Dorsal and lateral scales outlined with melanophores. Black spot on anterior portion of dorsal fin of males. Fins, except pectorals, with thin black margins. Paired fins and anal fin light yellow.

Leon Springs pupfish, *Cyprinodon bovinus*, female, 1.7 in (43 mm)

Leon Springs pupfish, *Cyprinodon bovinus*, male, 1.9 in (48 mm)

Leon Springs Pupfish

Cyprinodon bovinus Baird and Girard, 1853

RANGE: Leon Creek basin (Pecos County).

HABITAT: Creeks with pools and the edges of spring-fed marshes.

CHARACTERISTICS:

(1) Mouth small and terminal.

(2) Mandible with 2 pores.

(3) Belly fully scaled.

(4) Lateral region with dark brown blotches triangular or rectangular in shape; females with numerous small blotches on lower portion of lateral region.

(5) Lateral line absent; 23–26 lateral series scales.

DIMENSIONS: Up to 2.3 in (58 mm).

FIN COUNTS: Anal soft fin rays 7; dorsal soft fin rays 9–12; pelvic soft fin rays 18–23.

COLORATION: Dorsal region gray-brown; lateral region silver with dark brown blotches; ventral region white. Median fins dusky. Females with numerous small blotches on lower lateral region.

COMMENTS: This species is listed by the state as endangered.

Red River pupfish, *Cyprinodon rubrofluviatilis,* 2 in (51 mm)

Red River Pupfish

Cyprinodon rubrofluviatilis Fowler, 1916

RANGE: Upper Brazos River and the Red River basin as well as the Canadian and Colorado river basins as a result of introductions.

HABITAT: Headwaters, creeks, and rivers in pools and runs.

CHARACTERISTICS:

(1) Small, terminal mouth with tricuspid teeth.

(2) Slender body; greatest body depth goes more than 2.5 times into standard length, most notably in adults.

(3) Breast naked.

(4) Belly naked.

(5) Midlateral region with 8–11 dark triangular or rectangular blotches.

(6) Lateral line absent; 25–29 lateral series scales.

DIMENSIONS: Up to 2.3 in (58 mm).

FIN COUNTS: Anal soft fin rays 8–9; dorsal soft fin rays 9.

COLORATION: Dorsal region olive; lateral region olive with 8–11 dark vertical blotches; ventral region white. Breeding males with dorsal region of head iridescent green. Median fins yellow to orange, anal fins with red border, pelvic fins bright orange, and pectoral fins yellow.

Sheepshead minnow, *Cyprinodon variegatus,* male, 1.7 in (43 mm)

Sheepshead minnow, *Cyprinodon variegatus,* female, 1.6 in (41 mm)

Sheepshead Minnow

Cyprinodon variegatus Lacépède, 1809

RANGE: Mainly an estuarine species but can be found along coastal areas and will migrate upstream; the Trans-Pecos region as well as the upper Colorado and San Antonio river basins are the result of introductions.

HABITAT: Lakes, rivers, and creeks.

CHARACTERISTICS:

(1) Deep body; more slender body profile when found in lakes.

(2) Dark, triangle-shaped blotches (5–8); may be absent.

(3) Belly fully scaled.

(4) Lateral line absent; 22–28 lateral series scales.

(5) Large humeral scale.

DIMENSIONS: Up to 3 in (76 mm).

FIN COUNTS: Anal soft fin rays 9–11; dorsal soft fin rays 10–12.

COLORATION: Dorsal region green to blue-gray; lateral region olive-silver with 5–8 dark, triangle-shaped bars; ventral region white. Fins have a clear to pale yellow coloration. Breeding males are blue dorsally, while the cheek, breast, and belly have a brassy coloration. Fins of breeding males are orange with the caudal fin having a black posterior margin.

White bass, *Morone chrysops,*
11 in (279 mm)

White Bass

Morone chrysops (Rafinesque, 1820)

RANGE: Statewide, due to introductions, excluding the Trans-Canadian region

HABITAT: Usually found in lakes, ponds, and rivers in pools.

CHARACTERISTICS:

(1) Eyes with yellow coloration.

(2) Single tooth patch on tongue.

(3) Dark, horizontal stripes (4–7) on silver-white lateral region; may be less notable in specimens taken from turbid water; lines can be broken or offset.

(4) Second anal spine notably shorter than third anal spine.

(5) First dorsal fin with 9 spines; second dorsal fin with 1 spine.

(6) Pelvic fins with 1 spine.

(7) Anal fin with 3 spines.

(8) Lateral line scales: 51–60.

DIMENSIONS: Up to 20.7 in (526 mm) and 5.5 lbs (2.5 kg).

FIN COUNTS: Anal soft fin rays 11–13; dorsal soft fin rays 12–14; pectoral soft fin rays 15–17; pelvic soft fin rays 5.

COLORATION: Eyes with yellow tint. Dorsal region blue-gray; lateral region silver-white with 4–7 dark, horizontal stripes; ventral region white.

COMMENTS: The white bass can be distinguished from the yellow bass by its dorsal fins being separate as opposed to slightly connected by a membrane on the yellow bass, second anal spine notably shorter than third anal spine where the second and third anal spines are about equal length on yellow bass, 11–13 soft fin rays in the anal fin versus 9–10 soft anal fin rays on yellow bass, a single tooth patch on the tongue versus no tooth patch for yellow bass, and lateral region stripes being continuous versus offset just above the anal fin on yellow bass.

Yellow bass, *Morone mississippiensis,* 6 in (152 mm)

Yellow Bass

Morone mississippiensis Jordan and Eigenmann, 1887

RANGE: San Jacinto River basin north to the Red River basin.

HABITAT: Lakes, ponds, and rivers in pools and backwaters.

CHARACTERISTICS:

(1) Dark, horizontal stripes (5–7) on silver-yellow lateral region; stripes just above anal fin broken and offset.

(2) First and second dorsal fin united by membrane; may be torn on preserved specimens.

(3) Second anal spine about as long as third anal spine.

(4) First dorsal fin with 9 spines; second dorsal fin with 1 spine.

(5) Anal fin with 3 spines; second spine about same length as third spine.

(6) Pelvic fins with 1 spine.

(7) Lateral line scales: 49–51.

DIMENSIONS: Up to 18 in (457 mm) and 3.5 lbs (1.6 kg).

FIN COUNTS: Anal soft fin rays 9–10; dorsal soft fin rays 11–13; pelvic soft fin rays 5.

COLORATION: Dorsal region olive-gray; lateral region silver-yellow with 5–7 dark horizontal stripes broken and offset above anal fin. Breeding males are bright yellow.

Striped bass,
Morone saxatalis,
24 in (610 mm)

Striped Bass

Morone saxatilis (Walbaum, 1792)

RANGE: Introduced into reservoirs throughout much of the state.

HABITAT: Lakes, reservoirs, and rivers.

CHARACTERISTICS:

(1) Two parallel tooth patches on tongue.
(2) First and second dorsal fins separate.
(3) Dark, horizontal stripes (6–9) on silver-white lateral region; stripes are continuous and uninterrupted.
(4) Lateral line scales: 57–68.
(5) Second anal spine notably shorter than third anal spine.

DIMENSIONS: Up to 80 lbs (36 kg).

FIN COUNTS: Anal soft fin rays 9–13; dorsal soft fin rays 8–14 (on second dorsal fin); pectoral soft fin rays 15–17.

COLORATION: Dorsal region dark olive to blue-gray; lateral region silver-white with 6–9 dark, horizontal stripes and scattered brassy specks. Juveniles lack stripes and have vertical bars.

COMMENTS: The striped bass may be distinguished from the white bass and yellow bass by its two parallel tooth patches on the tongue and elongate body; body depth goes into standard length more than 3 times.

Rock bass, *Ambloplites rupestris,* 4.1 in (104 mm)

Rock Bass

Ambloplites rupestris (Rafinesque, 1817)

RANGE: San Marcos, Comal, and upper Guadalupe river basins (introduced).

HABITAT: Spring-fed lakes, creeks, and rivers with pools.

CHARACTERISTICS:

(1) Iris of eye red.

(2) Mouth large; lower jaw extends past middle of eye.

(3) Pharyngeal teeth sharp.

(4) Teeth present on tongue as well as vomer and palatine bones.

(5) Gill rakers moderately long; longest gill raker longer than pupil diameter.

(6) Opercle flaps short and inflexible.

(7) Pectoral fins short and rounded; do not reach beyond eye when bent forward.

(8) Scales with dark spots forming horizontal stripes on lateral region; stripes may be obscured by mottled coloration of lateral region.

(9) Dark mottling on dorsal and upper lateral region; most notable on juveniles.

(10) Dorsal fin with 10–13 spines.

(11) Anal fin with 5–6 spines.

(12) Anal fin with black margin, males only.

DIMENSIONS: Up to 17 in (432 mm).

FIN COUNTS: Anal soft fin rays 9–11; dorsal soft fin rays 10–13; pectoral soft fin rays 13–15.

COLORATION: Dorsal and upper lateral region dark green or brown with mottling. Spots on scales form horizontal stripes on middle and lower lateral regions; ventral region white. The median fins of rock bass are mottled with brown. Anal fin of males has black margin. Eyes have red irises.

COMMENTS: The rock bass can be distinguished from the green sunfish and warmouth by its 5–6 anal spines versus the 3 anal spines of the green sunfish and the warmouth.

Flier, *Centrarchus macropterus,* adult, 5 in (127 mm)

Flier, *Centrarchus macropterus,* juvenile, 2 in (51 mm)

Flier

Centrarchus macropterus (Lacépède, 1801)

RANGE: Sabine, Neches, and San Jacinto river drainages.

HABITAT: Lakes, ponds, sloughs, rivers, and creeks in backwaters and pools.

CHARACTERISTICS:

(1) Mouth medium sized; lower jaw almost reaches middle of eye.

(2) Dark suborbital bars

(3) Teeth on vomer, palatine, and pterygoid bones; 2 tooth patches on tongue.

(4) Dorsal fin with 11–13 spines.

(5) Anal fin with 7–8 spines; anal fin almost as large as dorsal fin.

(6) Lateral line scales: 36–42.

(7) Brown spots on scales form horizontal rows on lateral region.

(8) Median fins with small, light colored spots.

DIMENSIONS: Up to 8 in (203 mm) and 1 lb (0.5 kg).

FIN COUNTS: Anal soft fin rays 13–15; dorsal soft fin rays 12–15; pectoral soft fin rays 12–14.

COLORATION: Head with dark suborbital bars. Dorsal and upper lateral region olive-green; lateral region with brown spots on scales forming horizontal rows; ventral region yellow. Median fins with small, light colored spots. Juveniles have a large, black blotch at posterior portion of dorsal fin that fades as they mature.

Redbreast sunfish, *Lepomis auritus,* juvenile, 2.9 in (74 mm)

Redbreast sunfish, *Lepomis auritus,* adult, 7 in (178 mm)

Redbreast Sunfish
Lepomis Auritus (Linnaeus, 1758)

RANGE: Statewide, except for far west Texas and Panhandle (introduced).

HABITAT: Lakes, rivers, and creeks in pools.

CHARACTERISTICS:

(1) Opercle flaps on adults long and flexible. Flexible opercle flaps black to posterior margin with dorsal and ventral margins white.

(2) Teeth present on palatine bones.

(3) Gill rakers short.

(4) Pectoral fins short, not reaching beyond eye when bent forward.

(5) Dorsal fin with 10–11 spines.

(6) Lateral line scales: 39–54.

(7) Anal fin with 3 spines.

DIMENSIONS: Up to 12.7 in (323 mm) and 1.2 lbs (0.54 kg).

FIN COUNTS: Anal soft fin rays 9–10; dorsal soft fin rays 10–12; pectoral soft fin rays 13–15.

COLORATION: Opercle flap black to posterior margin with dorsal and ventral margins blue. Dorsal and lateral region dark olive; ventral region red to yellow. Cheeks and opercle have blue wavy streaks. Breeding male redbreast sunfish has bright red chest and breast. Juveniles have a dark posterior margin on the caudal fin.

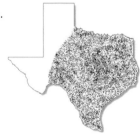

Green sunfish, *Lepomis cyanellus,* adult, 6.5 in (165 mm)

Green sunfish, *Lepomis cyanellus,* juvenile, 2.8 in (71 mm)

Green Sunfish
Lepomis cyanellus (Rafinesque, 1819)

RANGE: Statewide.

HABITAT: Lakes, ponds, and creeks in pools and backwaters.

CHARACTERISTICS:

(1) Mouth large; lower jaw extends to about middle of eye.

(2) Teeth present on palatine and vomer bones.

(3) Pharyngeal teeth blunt and conical.

(4) Gill rakers long and thin; longest gill rakers as long as diameter of pupil.

(5) Opercle flaps dark with white or yellow-orange margin; opercle flaps inflexible.

(6) Pectoral fins short and rounded; do not reach beyond eye when bent forward.

(7) Dark, blotch on posterior portion of dorsal and anal fin; blotches may be faded or absent.

(8) Dorsal fin with 9–11 spines.

(9) Pelvic fins with 1 spine.

(10) Lateral line scales: 41–52.

(11) Caudal, pelvic, and anal fins with white, yellow, or orange margins.

(12) Anal fin with 3 spines.

DIMENSIONS: Up to 10 in (254 mm) and 1.2 lbs (0.54 kg).

FIN COUNTS: Anal soft fin rays 8–11; dorsal soft fin rays 9–12; pectoral soft fin rays 13–15.

COLORATION: Sides of head with iridescent blue or green mottling. Dorsal and lateral region brown to bluish-green with dark, mottled vertical bars; ventral region yellow to yellow-orange. Large, dark blotch on posterior portion of dorsal and anal fin base. Dorsal, anal, and pelvic fins with white to yellow-orange margins. Opercles with large black spot and a yellow or white margin.

COMMENTS: The green sunfish can be distinguished from the rock bass by its 3 anal spines versus the 5–6 anal spines on rock bass. It can be distinguished from the warmouth by its lack of teeth on the tongue versus patch of teeth on the tongue of the warmouth.

Warmouth, *Lepomis gulosus,* adult, 8.6 in (218 mm)

Warmouth

Lepomis gulosus (Cuvier, 1829)

RANGE: Statewide, except for extreme northern Panhandle area.

HABITAT: Lakes, ponds, swamps, rivers, and creeks.

CHARACTERISTICS:

(1) Eyes red.

(2) Mouth large; upper jaw extends to about middle of eye or beyond.

(3) Teeth on tongue and pterygoid bones.

(4) Large supramaxilla.

(5) Gill rakers long; longest gill rakers usually as long as diameter of pupil.

(6) Brown and yellow stripes running from eyes to margin of opercles.

(7) Dorsal fin with 10–11 spines.

(8) Pelvic fins with 1 spine.

(9) Lateral line with 35–44 scales.

(10) Anal fin with 3 spines.

DIMENSIONS: Up to 10.5 in (268 mm) and 1.7 lbs (0.77 kg).

FIN COUNTS: Anal soft fin rays 8–10; dorsal soft fin rays 9–10; pectoral soft fin rays 12–13.

COLORATION: Head with brown and yellow stripes running from eyes to gill cover margin. Dorsal and lateral region olive-brown with mottled brown vertical bars; ventral region light yellow. Fins with dark mottling pattern. Juveniles with dark vertical bars on lateral region. Breeding males with orange spot at base of last three rays of dorsal fin.

COMMENTS: See comments on the green sunfish and the rock bass.

Orangespotted sunfish, *Lepomis humilis,* 3 in (76 mm)

Orangespotted Sunfish
Lepomis humilis (Girard, 1858)

RANGE: Colorado River basin north to the Red River basin. As a result of introductions they can also be found in other areas of the state.

HABITAT: Lakes, rivers, and creeks.

(1) Head pointed and small.

(2) Mouth fairly large; upper jaw reaches past anterior edge of eye.

(3) Teeth on palatine bones.

(4) Pharyngeal teeth sharp.

(5) Gill rakers moderately long; longest rakers about one-third the diameter of eye.

(6) Opercle flaps dark, with thick white margin; opercle flaps flexible.

(7) Pectoral fins short and rounded to moderately long and pointed, reaching to about anterior edge of eye.

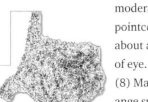

(8) Males with orange spots on lateral region; females and juveniles with brown spots.

(9) Dorsal fin with 9–11 spines.

(10) Pelvic fins with 1 spine.

(11) Lateral line scales: 32–42; lateral line may be incomplete.

(12) Anal fin with 3 spines.

DIMENSIONS: Up to 6 in (152 mm).

FIN COUNTS: Anal soft fin rays 7–9; dorsal soft fin rays 10–11; pectoral soft fin rays 14–15; pelvic soft fin rays 5.

COLORATION: Opercle flap dark with white margin. Dorsal and lateral region silver-green with orange spots; ventral region white. Females and juveniles with brown spots. Juvenile orangespotted sunfish lack orange or brown spots and have vertical bars on the lateral region. Breeding male orangespotted sunfish have bright orange spots on lateral region; belly and median fins bright red-orange; anal and pelvic fins with black margins; sides of head with iridescent blue streaks.

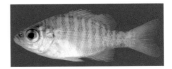

Bluegill, *Lepomis macrochirus*, juvenile, 1.7 in (43 mm)

Bluegill, *Lepomis macrochirus,* adult, 8.5 in (216 mm)

Bluegill

Lepomis macrochirus Rafinesque, 1819

RANGE: Statewide.

HABITAT: Lakes, ponds, and swamps, as well as rivers and creeks in pools.

CHARACTERISTICS:

(1) Mouth small, upper jaw not reaching past anterior edge of eye.

(2) Gill rakers long, thin, and straight; longest gill rakers more than half the diameter of eye.

(3) Opercle flaps dark to margin, somewhat long, and flexible.

(4) Pectoral fins long and moderately to sharply pointed, usually reaches beyond anterior edge of eye when bent forward.

(5) Dark blotch on posterior portion of dorsal fin; may be faded in large adults.

(6) Lateral region with 6–7 dark vertical bars on adults, 9–12 on juveniles. Vertical bars maybe absent on large adults or those taken from turbid water.

(7) Dorsal fin with 10–11 spines.

(8) Pelvic fins with 1 spine.

(9) Lateral line scales: 39–44.

(10) Anal fin with 3 spines.

DIMENSIONS: Up to 16 in (406 mm).

FIN COUNTS: Anal soft fin rays 11–12; dorsal soft fin rays 10–12; pectoral soft fin rays 13–14; pelvic soft fin rays 5.

COLORATION: Opercle flaps dark to margins, with the chin and lower portion of operculum blue. Dorsal and upper-lateral region dark olive-green; lateral region with 6–7 dark vertical bars on adults, 9–12 bars on juveniles; ventral region yellow or red-orange. Dark blotch on posterior portion of dorsal fin. Breeding males have darker colors, and fins become darkly pigmented.

Redspotted sunfish, *Lepomis miniatus*, 4.1 in (104 mm)

Redspotted Sunfish

Lepomis miniatus (Jordan, 1877)

RANGE: Statewide, excluding the Panhandle and far west Texas.

HABITAT: Ponds, lakes, swamps, and rivers and creeks in pools.

CHARACTERISTICS:

(1) Mouth small; upper jaw reaches past anterior edge of eye.

(2) Gill rakers medium length; may be shorter in some adults.

(3) Opercle flaps dark, with thin white or yellow margin. Opercle flaps inflexible.

(4) Pectoral fins short and rounded; do not reach past eye when bent forward.

(5) Lateral region with black spots on scales forming horizontal lines. Spots may be red or orange.

(6) Dorsal fin with 10 spines.

(7) Pelvic fins with 1 spine.

(8) Lateral line scales: 34–40.

(9) Anal fin with 3 spines.

DIMENSIONS: Up to 6 in (152 mm).

FIN COUNTS: Anal soft fin rays 10–11; dorsal soft fin rays 10–12; pectoral soft fin rays 13–15.

COLORATION: Head and face black; dark opercle with a white or yellow margin. Dorsal and lateral region dark blue or olive with brassy sheen; lateral region has black or red or orange spots on scales forming horizontal lines; ventral region yellow or pale white.

Bantam sunfish,
Lepomis symmetricus, 2.7 in
(69 mm)

Bantam Sunfish

Lepomis symmetricus Forbes, 1883

RANGE: Colorado River basin north to the Red River basin.

HABITAT: Swamps, ponds, lakes, and sloughs.

CHARACTERISTICS:

(1) Mouth small; upper jaw does not extend past eye.

(2) Opercle flaps dark, with light colored posterior margin; opercle flaps inflexible.

(3) Gill rakers long, about 6 times the width of gill raker base.

(4) Dark blotch on posterior portion of dorsal fin, which may be faded or absent on adults; pale margin surrounds dark blotch on juveniles.

(5) Pectoral fins short and rounded or moderately long and pointed; do not reach past eye when bent forward.

(6) Dorsal fin with 9–11 spines.

(7) Pelvic fins with 1 spine.

(8) Anal fin with 3 spines.

(9) Lateral line incomplete or interrupted; 30–38 lateral series scales.

(10) Base of scales with dark spots form horizontal lines or faint vertical stripes on lateral region.

DIMENSIONS: Up to 3.5 in (89 mm).

FIN COUNTS: Anal soft fin rays 9–11; dorsal soft fin rays 9–12; pectoral soft fin rays 11–13.

COLORATION: Head and cheeks dark with dark opercle flaps having a thin, light colored posterior margin. Dorsal and lateral region dark green; lateral region scales have dark spot at bases forming horizontal lines or faint vertical bars; ventral region yellow-brown. Dark blotch on posterior portion of dorsal fin. Breeding males have darker colors.

Dollar sunfish, *Lepomis marginatus*, 4.2 in (107 mm)

Dollar Sunfish

Lepomis marginatus (Holbrook, 1855)

RANGE: Navasota River basin eastward to the Sabine and Sulphur river basins.

HABITAT: Swamps, creeks, and rivers.

CHARACTERISTICS:

(1) Mouth small; upper jaw does not reach past middle of eye.

(2) Gill rakers short; longest gill rakers not more than 2 times the width of gill raker base.

(3) Opercle flaps dark, with white or silver spots and thin green or white margin; opercle flaps flexible.

(4) Pectoral fins short and rounded; do not reach past eye when bent forward.

(5) Dorsal fin with 9–11 spines.

(6) Pelvic fins with 1 spine.

(7) Lateral line with 32–42 scales.

(8) Anal fin with 3 spines.

DIMENSIONS: Up to 5 in (127 mm).

FIN COUNTS: Anal soft fin rays 9–10; dorsal soft fin rays 10–12; pectoral soft fin rays 11–13.

COLORATION: Cheeks with wavy blue lines; opercle flaps dark, with white or silver dots and thin green or white margin. Dorsal and lateral region blue-green with specks of yellow or orange; lateral region scales with dark centers and faint edges; ventral region yellow or orange.

COMMENTS: The dollar sunfish can be distinguished from the longear sunfish by its lower number of cheek scale rows (3–5 rows versus 5–7 rows for the longear sunfish) and usually having 12 rays (rarely 13) in the pectoral fins (versus 13–15 rays in the pectoral fins of the longear sunfish).

Longear sunfish, *Lepomis megalotis,* juvenile, 2.3 in (58 mm)

Longear sunfish, *Lepomis megalotis,* adult, 6.5 in (165 mm)

Longear Sunfish

Lepomis megalotis (Rafinesque, 1820)

RANGE: Statewide, excluding the headwaters of the Canadian and Brazos Rivers.

HABITAT: Headwaters of rivers and creeks.

CHARACTERISTICS:

(1) Mouth fairly small; upper jaw does not reach past middle of eye.

(2) Blue to green stripes from mouth and eyes running to the cheek and opercle.

(3) Gill rakers short.

(4) Opercle flap dark with red or white margin; opercle flaps flexible.

(5) Pectoral fins short and rounded; do not reach eye when bent forward.

(6) Dorsal fin with 10–12 spines.

(7) Pelvic fins with 1 spine.

(8) Lateral line scales: 33–45.

(9) Anal fin with 3 spines.

DIMENSIONS: Up to 9.5 in (241 mm).

FIN COUNTS: Anal soft fin rays 9–10; dorsal soft fin rays 10–12; pectoral soft fin rays 13–15.

COLORATION: Opercle flap dark with red or white margin and head with green or blue stripes from mouth and eyes to cheek and opercle. Dorsal and lateral region olive, occasionally with specks of yellow or green; ventral region yellow or orange. Breeding males are iridescent green or turquoise on dorsal and lateral regions and bright red-orange on ventral region; fins are red-brown.

COMMENTS: See comments on the dollar sunfish.

Redear sunfish, *Lepomis microlophus*, 8.5 in (216 mm)

Redear Sunfish

Lepomis microlophus (Gunther, 1859)

RANGE: Mainly found in eastern portions of the state, but may be found statewide due to introductions.
HABITAT: Ponds, swamps, lakes, and rivers in pools.
CHARACTERISTICS:
(1) Mouth small; upper jaw does not extend past front of eye.
(2) Pharyngeal teeth molarlike.
(3) Gill rakers short and blunt; may appear crooked.
(4) Opercle flaps dark, with posterior margin being red or orange; may not be notable on juveniles. Opercle flaps inflexible.

(5) Lateral region mottled with brown spots; may form checkered pattern or vertical bars.
(6) Pectoral fins long and pointed; usually reach far past eye when bent forward.
(7) Dorsal fin with 9–11 spines.
(8) Pelvic fins with 1 spine.
(9) Lateral line scales: 34–43.
(10) Anal fin with 3 spines.
DIMENSIONS: Up to 13.2 in (335 mm) and 3 lbs (1.4 kg).
FIN COUNTS: Anal soft fin rays 9–11; dorsal soft fin rays 10–12; pectoral soft fin rays 12–14.
COLORATION: Dark opercular flaps with red or orange posterior margin. Dorsal region olive-green; lateral region silvery, mottled with brown spots; ventral region yellow. Juveniles have vertical bars on lateral region.

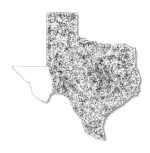

Smallmouth bass, *Micropterus dolomieu,* adult, 9 in (229 mm)

Smallmouth bass, *Micropterus dolomieu,* juvenile, 3 in (76 mm)

Smallmouth Bass

Micropterus dolomieu Lacépède, 1802

RANGE: Primarily found in portions of the Edwards Plateau, but may be found statewide as the result of introductions.

HABITAT: Lakes as well as rivers in runs, riffles, and pools.

CHARACTERISTICS:

(1) Mouth moderately large; upper jaw does not reach past posterior margin of eye.

(2) Dark bars (3) on each cheek.

(3) Spiny and rayed portions of dorsal fin broadly joined with shallow notch between them.

(4) Membranes at the base of the rayed portions of dorsal and anal fins with small scales.

(5) Lateral region with 8–16 dark vertical bars.

(6) Lower lateral region with smoky coloration and scattered small, dark spots; spots may be absent.

(7) Dorsal fin with 9–10 spines.

(8) Lateral line scales: 67–81.

9) Anal fin with 3 spines.

DIMENSIONS: Up to 20 in (508 mm) and 4 lbs (1.8 kg).

FIN COUNTS: Anal soft fin rays 10–12; dorsal soft fin rays 12–15.

COLORATION: Cheeks with 3 dark bars. Dorsal region olive-brown to bronze with dark mottling, which may be absent; lateral region olive-brown to bronze with 8–16 dark vertical bars and mottling as well as scattered dark spots on lower lateral region (the bars, mottling, and spots may all be absent); ventral region a smoky color with scattered small, dark spots. Juveniles (less than 6 inches) have a caudal fin with an orange base, black submarginal stripe, and yellow to white margin.

COMMENTS: The smallmouth bass can be distinguished from the spotted bass by its lack of a tooth patch on the tongue and the lack of horizontal rows of dark spots on scales on lower lateral region versus the tooth patch and horizontal rows of dark scale spots on lower lateral region on the spotted bass.

Spotted bass,
Micropterus punctulatus,
10 in (254 mm)

Spotted Bass

Micropterus punctulatus (Rafinesque, 1819)

RANGE: Guadalupe River basin northeastward to the Red River basin.
HABITAT: Lakes, creeks, and rivers in runs and pools.
CHARACTERISTICS:
(1) Mouth moderately large; upper jaw does not reach past middle of pupil.
(2) Tooth patch on tongue.
(3) Spiny and rayed portions of dorsal fin broadly joined with shallow notch between them.
(4) Membranes at the base of the rayed portions of dorsal and anal fins with small scales.
(5) Midlateral stripe of dark blotches.

(6) Lower lateral region scales with dark spots forming horizontal rows.
(7) Dorsal fin with 10 spines.
(8) Lateral line scales: 55–71.
(9) Anal fin with 3 spines.
(10) Dark basicaudal spot; most notable in juveniles.
DIMENSIONS: Up to 15 in (381 mm) and 3 lbs (1.4 kg).
FIN COUNTS: Anal soft fin rays 9–11; dorsal soft fin rays 11–14; pectoral soft fin rays 15–16.
COLORATION: Dorsal region olive-green with dark mottling; lateral region with midlateral stripe of dark blotches; lower lateral region scales with dark spots forming horizontal rows; ventral region white. Breeding males have eye irises that are red. Juveniles (less than 6 inches) have a caudal fin with a red to orange base, white margin, and a gray or black submarginal stripe.
COMMENTS: To distinguish the spotted bass from the largemouth bass and the Guadalupe bass see the comments section for each of these species.

Largemouth bass, *Micropterus salmoides*, adult, 11 in (279 mm)

Largemouth bass, *Micropterus salmoides*, juvenile, 3.2 in (81 mm)

Largemouth Bass

Micropterus salmoides (Lacépède, 1802)

RANGE: Statewide.

HABITAT: Lakes, impoundments, ponds, swamps, and rivers and creeks in pools and backwaters.

CHARACTERISTICS:

(1) Mouth large; adult, upper jaw reaches past posterior margin of eye.

(2) Spiny and rayed portions of dorsal fin narrowly joined with a deep notch between them.

(3) Dark midlateral stripe from tip of snout to caudal fin base; may be a series of blotches anteriorly or may be faded or absent on specimens from turbid water.

(4) Dorsal fin with usually 9 spines.

(5) Lateral line scales: 59–72.

(6) Anal fin with 3 spines.

DIMENSIONS: Up to 38 in (965 mm) and 21 lbs (9.5 kg) or more.

FIN COUNTS: Anal soft fin rays 11–12; dorsal soft fin rays 12–14; pectoral soft fin rays 14–15.

COLORATION: Dorsal region olive to dark green with dark mottling, which may not be notable; lateral region olive to green with dark midlateral stripe with smooth edges from tip of snout to caudal fin base, which may be broken up into blotches anteriorly; lower lateral region often with scattered dark spots; ventral region white with scattered dark spots that are not always present. Juveniles (less than 6 inches) have a dark caudal spot and a caudal fin with a gray posterior margin while the remainder of the fin is whitish orange.

COMMENTS: The largemouth bass can be distinguished from spotted bass and Guadalupe bass by its large mouth (upper jaw reaching past posterior edge of eye in adults versus upper jaw not reaching past middle of eye in spotted and Guadalupe bass); lack of tooth patch on tongue (tooth patch on tongue of spotted and Guadalupe bass); spiny and rayed portions of dorsal fin narrowly joined with deep notch between them (broadly joined with shallow notch for spotted and Guadalupe bass).

Guadalupe bass, *Micropterus treculii,* adult, 9 in (229 mm)

Guadalupe bass, *Micropterus treculii,* juvenile, 3.2 in (81 mm)

Guadalupe Bass

Micropterus treculii (Vaillant and Bocourt, 1874)

RANGE: Brazos, Guadalupe, Colorado, and San Antonio river basins. Guadalupe bass found in the Nueces River basin are the result of introductions.

HABITAT: Rivers and creeks in pools, riffles, and runs.

CHARACTERISTICS:

(1) Mouth moderately large; upper jaw does not reach past middle of eye.

(2) Tooth patch on tongue.

(3) Spiny and rayed portions of dorsal fin broadly joined with a shallow notch between them.

(4) Lower dorsal and lateral region scales with dark spots forming horizontal rows.

(5) Dark midlateral stripe obscured by 10–12 vertical bars; most notable on juveniles.

(6) Dorsal fin with 10 spines.

(7) Lateral line scales: 55–71.

(8) Anal fin with 3 spines.

DIMENSIONS: Up to up 18.2 in (462 mm) and 3.7 lbs (1.7 kg).

FIN COUNTS: Anal soft fin rays 9–11; dorsal soft fin rays 11–14; pectoral soft fin rays 15–16.

COLORATION: Dorsal region olive-green with dark spots on scales of lower dorsal region forming horizontal rows; lateral region with dark midlateral stripe obscured by 10–12 vertical bars (bars most notable on juveniles); lower lateral region with dark scale spots forming horizontal rows; ventral region white. Juvenile Guadalupe bass have 10–12 dark vertical bars and caudal spot.

COMMENTS: The Guadalupe bass has been designated as the official state fish of Texas. It should be noted that hybrid forms of Guadalupe bass and spotted bass or Guadalupe and smallmouth bass do exist.

White crappie, *Pomoxis
annularis,* 8 in (203 mm)

White Crappie
Pomoxis annularis Rafinesque, 1818

RANGE: Statewide, excluding portions of the Trans-Pecos.

HABITAT: Lakes, ponds, and rivers and creeks in pools and backwaters.

CHARACTERISTICS:

(1) Small head.

(2) Large mouth; upper jaw reaches past the middle of eye.

(3) Length of dorsal fin base less than distance from dorsal fin origin to posterior edge of eye.

(4) Lateral region with dark blotches forming 5–10 vertical bars, widest near dorsal region; specimens taken from turbid water might not show barring.

(5) Dorsal fin usually with 6 spines.

(6) Lateral line scales: 38–45.

(7) Anal fin with 6 spines.

DIMENSIONS: Up to 21 in (533 mm).

FIN COUNTS: Anal soft fin rays 17–18; dorsal soft fin rays 13–15.

COLORATION: Dorsal region dark olive; lateral region silver with dark blotches forming 5–10 vertical bars. Median fins of white crappie are striped and mottled with black. Breeding males have head and breast almost black.

COMMENTS: The white crappie can be distinguished from the black crappie by its 6 dorsal spines versus 7–8 spines for black crappie, dorsal fin base length less than the distance from the dorsal fin origin to the posterior edge of eye orbit versus dorsal fin base length greater than the distance from dorsal fin origin to posterior edge of eye for black crappie, and dark blotches forming 5–10 vertical bars on the lateral region versus dark blotches and speckles scattered on the lateral region of the black crappie.

Black crappie, *Pomoxis nigro-maculatus,* 10 in (254 mm)

Black Crappie

Pomoxis nigromaculatus (Lesueur, 1829)

RANGE: Central Texas and eastward to the Sabine River basin.
HABITAT: Lakes, ponds, sloughs, and creeks in pools and backwaters.
CHARACTERISTICS:
(1) Head small.
(2) Mouth large; upper jaw reaches past middle of eye.
(3) Length of dorsal fin base reaches from eye to dorsal fin origin.
(4) Lateral region with scattered dark blotches and speckles; markings rarely form vertical bars.
(5) Dorsal fin with 7–8 spines.
(6) Lateral line scales: 38–44.
(7) Anal fin with 6 spines.
DIMENSIONS: Up to 19.2 in (488 mm).
FIN COUNTS: Anal soft fin rays 17–19; dorsal soft fin rays 15–16.
COLORATION: Dorsal region dark olive with reflections of green; lateral region silver with scattered dark blotches and speckles; ventral region silver-white. Black crappie median fins have black mottling and barring. Breeding males have the above colors in darker shades with head and breast almost black.
COMMENTS: See comments for white crappie.

Western sand
darter, *Ammo-
crypta clara,* 2 in
(51 mm)

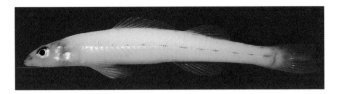

Western Sand Darter

Ammocrypta clara Jordan and Meek,
1885

RANGE: Neches, Sabine, and Red
river basins.
HABITAT: Rivers and creeks with
runs.
CHARACTERISTICS:
(1) Cheek and opercle partly scaled.
(2) Opercle with large spine.
(3) Nape with few or no scales.
(4) Belly, prepectoral area, and breast
    unscaled.
(5) Dorsal region with small, dark
    spots forming a thin middorsal line
(6) Lateral region with faint dashes
    that may be absent. Dashes may
    connect to form a midlateral stripe.
(7) Dorsal fin with 9–13 spines.
(8) Anal fin with 1 spine.
(9) Lateral line scales: 63–84.
DIMENSIONS: Up to 2.3 in
(59 mm).

FIN COUNTS: Anal soft fin rays
8–11; dorsal soft fin rays 9–13.
COLORATION: Dorsal region pale
yellow with small dark spots forming
a thin middorsal line; lateral region
translucent with faint dashes that
may connect to form a midlateral
stripe; ventral region silvery white.

Scaly sand darter, *Ammocrypta vivax,* 2.4 in (61 mm)

Scaly Sand Darter
Ammocrypta vivax Hay, 1882

RANGE: San Jacinto, Trinity, Neches, Sabine, and Red river basins.
HABITAT: Rivers and creeks in runs.
CHARACTERISTICS:
(1) Cheeks and preopercles scaled.
(2) Thin, dark stripes on spiny dorsal fin.
(3) Dorsal region with 10–15 dark spots that may extend onto lateral region.
(4) Nape partly scaled.
(5) Scales on prepectoral area and edges of breast (scales embedded).
(6) Midline of belly scaleless.
(7) Midlateral region with 9–16 dark blotches that are taller than wide.
(8) First dorsal fin with 8–14 spines.
(9) Anal fin with 1 spine.
(10) Lateral line slightly (or not at all) bent downward posteriorly with 58–79 scales.
(11) Thin, dark stripes on caudal fin.
DIMENSIONS: Up to 2.7 in (69 mm).
FIN COUNTS: Anal soft fin rays 7–10; dorsal soft fin rays 9–12; pectoral soft fin rays 7–13.
COLORATION: Body pale yellow to white. Dorsal region with 10–15 dark spots; lateral region with 9–16 dark blotches. The dorsal and caudal fins have dark stripes while the anal, pectoral, and pelvic fins have dark pigment along the rays.

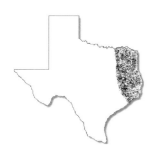

Redspot darter,
Etheostoma artesiae,
breeding adult, 3.2 in
(81 mm)

Redspot darter,
Etheostoma artesiae,
nonbreeding adult 3 in
(76 mm)

Redspot Darter

Etheostoma artesiae (Hay, 1881)

RANGE: San Jacinto River basin northeast to the Sabine River basin.
HABITAT: Headwaters, rivers, and creeks, in pools, riffles, and runs.
CHARACTERISTICS:
(1) Orbital bars notable.
(2) Cheeks scaled or unscaled.
(3) Mouth terminal.
(4) Frenum present.
(5) Gill membranes moderately connected.
(6) Nape and opercle partly to fully scaled.
(7) Dark humeral spots posterior to opercle.
(8) Breast usually unscaled.
(9) Lateral line incomplete; lateral series scales: 45–75, with 34–68 pored.
(10) Lateral region with red or yellow dots along with blue or brown vertical bars; may not be noticeable.
(11) Small, dark caudal spots (3), aligned vertically.
(12) Anal fin with 2 spines.
DIMENSIONS: Up to 3.5 in (89 mm).
FIN COUNTS: Anal soft fin rays 6–9; dorsal soft fin rays 11–16; pectoral soft fin rays 12–14; pelvic soft fin rays.
COLORATION: Dorsal region olive with 8–10 brown saddle blotches; dorsal and lateral region with brown mottling pattern; lateral region with red (males) and yellow (females) dots along with blue (males) or brown (females) vertical bars, which are most notable posteriorly. Dorsal fin of males with red base band, with a red-yellow band medially and a blue margin. Anal and caudal fins have a red base band with blue margins. First dorsal fins of females are spotted with a red-orange submarginal band; second dorsal fin has dark brown bands. Breeding males have bright red spots on lateral region, blue breast, red-orange belly, red and blue bands in median fins; pelvic and pectoral fins are blue.

Mud darter, *Etheostoma asprigene*, 2.3 in (58 mm)

Mud Darter

Etheostoma asprigene (Forbes, 1878)

RANGE: Neches River drainage basin north to the Red River basin.
HABITAT: Rivers and creeks in riffles.
CHARACTERISTICS:
(1) Cheeks and opercles scaled.
(2) Dark preorbital and suborbital bars; the latter may be faint in some specimens.
(3) Nape with scales.
(4) Breast without scales.
(5) Belly scaled; males may lack belly scales anteriorly.
(6) Mottling pattern on nape and anterior lateral region.
(7) Dorsal region with 6–10 dark blotches.
(8) Upper lateral region with horizontal lines.

(9) Posterior lateral region with 6–8 dark vertical bars.
(10) Dorsal fin with 10–11 spines.
(11) Anal fin with 2 spines.
(12) Lateral line incomplete; lateral series scales: 44–54, with 31–44 pored.
(13) Small, dark caudal spots (3).
DIMENSIONS: Up to 2.7 in (69 mm).
FIN COUNTS: Anal soft fin rays 7–9; dorsal soft fin rays 12–14.
COLORATION: Head and body olive-brown; head with dark preorbital and suborbital bars. Dorsal region with 6–10 dark blotches; nape and anterior lateral region with brown mottled pattern; upper lateral region with horizontal lines; posterior lateral region with 6–8 dark vertical bars and 3 caudal spots. The first dorsal fin has a broad, black basal stripe, a thin red-orange submarginal stripe, and a blue margin; the second dorsal fin has a wide orange stripe (or brown spots), and the caudal fin has rows of dark spots with some orange coloration. Breeding males have an orange belly, orange between vertical bars, blue-green anal fin, and blue pelvic fins.

Bluntnose darter,
Etheostoma chloroso-
mum, 2.1 in
(53 mm)

Bluntnose Darter

Etheostoma chlorosomum (Hay, 1881)

RANGE: Guadalupe River basin northward to the Red River basin.

HABITAT: Lakes, ponds, and swamps, as well as rivers and creeks in pools and backwaters.

CHARACTERISTICS:

(1) Dark postorbital spots and preorbital and suborbital bars; preorbital bars extend around front of snout.

(2) Snout extremely blunt.

(3) Nape unscaled to partly scaled.

(4) Opercles and cheeks scaled.

(5) Breast partly to fully scaled; scales may be embedded.

(6) Belly fully scaled; may be partly scaled, with scales on the posterior portion of belly and scaleless anteriorly.

(7) Dorsal region with about 6 saddle blotches, usually faint.

(8) Lateral region with dark X- or M-shaped markings.

(9) Dorsal fin with 8–11 spines.

(10) Lateral line incomplete; lateral series scales: 49–60, with 4–40 pored. Lateral line usually terminates below second dorsal fin.

(11) Anal fin with 1 spine.

(12) Small, dark caudal spot.

DIMENSIONS: Up to 2.5 in (64 mm).

FIN COUNTS: Anal soft fin rays 7–9; dorsal soft fin rays 9–12; pectoral soft fin rays 12–14.

COLORATION: Head with preorbital bars that extend (and connect) around snout in addition to dark suborbital bars and postorbital spots; lateral region greenish-yellow with dark X- and M-shaped markings and a small dark caudal spot; ventral region white. Dorsal and caudal fins with light brown stripes; other fins are colorless. Breeding males have the above colors in a darker shade, with the operculums having a metallic green coloration and the first dorsal fin with black stripes notable anteriorly.

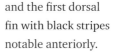

Fountain darter, *Etheostoma fonticola,* breeding adult,
1.1 in (28 mm)

Fountain darter, *Etheostoma fonticola,* nonbreeding adult,
1.0 in (25 mm)

Fountain Darter

Etheostoma fonticola (Jordan and
Gilbert, 1886)

RANGE: Upper portions of the San
Marcos and Comal Rivers.
HABITAT: Spring-fed rivers.
CHARACTERISTICS:
(1) Dark orbital bars.
(2) Nape unscaled.
(3) Cheeks unscaled.
(4) Opercles usually partly scaled.
(5) Prepectoral and parietal areas
unscaled.
(6) Breast unscaled and belly partly
scaled; scales on posterior portion
of belly with anterior portion unscaled.
(7) Dorsal and lateral region with
scattered dark spots; 7–8 saddle
blotches may be present on the
dorsal region

(8) Midlateral region
with dark dashes
that may appear as
blotches on breeding
males.

(9) First dorsal fin with 6–8 spines
(usually 6).
(10) Lateral line incomplete; lateral
series scales: 31–37, with 0–6 pored.
(11) Anal fin with 1 spine.
(12) Dark caudal spots (3); may be
absent.
DIMENSIONS: Up to 1.7 in
(43 mm).
FIN COUNTS: Anal soft fin rays
5–8; dorsal soft fin rays 10–13;
pectoral soft fin rays 8–11.
COLORATION: Head with dark
orbital bars. Dorsal and lateral regions
olive with dusky dorsal saddle blotches in addition to scattered dark spots
as well as 3 caudal spots; ventral region white. The first dorsal fin of males
has a dusky base, red median stripe,
and a thin, dusky margin. The first
dorsal fin of females is mostly clear.
The second dorsal fin and caudal fin of
males have light brown stripes while
the remaining fins are clear; pigmentation may run along fin rays.
COMMENTS: This species is listed
by the state as endangered.

Swamp darter, *Etheostoma fusiforme*, 1.7 in (43 mm)

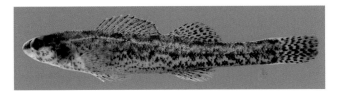

Swamp Darter

Etheostoma fusiforme (Girard, 1854)

RANGE: Cypress Creek drainage in northeast Texas.

HABITAT: Usually found in vegetation of standing or flowing waters with a sand or mud substrate.

CHARACTERISTICS:

(1) Head small; thin suborbital bar present.

(2) Mouth small.

(3) Distance from angle of gill cover greater than one-half the head length.

(4) Dorsal region usually with 9 saddle blotches that may be absent with dark green mottling in its place.

(5) Nape fully scaled.

(6) Cheeks fully scaled.

(7) Top of head fully scaled.

(8) Breast and belly fully scaled.

(9) Cheek and opercle with small dark spots.

(10) Gill membranes moderately joined across the throat.

11) Lateral line incomplete and strongly arched (appears as a short stripe); lateral series scales: 40–63, with 0–37 pored.

(12) Midlateral region with 9–12 small, dark rectangular blotches.

(13) First dorsal fin with 8–13 spines.

(14) Anal fin with 2 spines.

(15) Dark basicaudal spots (3).

DIMENSIONS: Up to 2.2 in (59 mm).

FIN COUNTS: Anal soft fin rays 5–10; dorsal soft fin rays 8–13.

COLORATION: Head with thin, dark suborbital bar; dorsal region green to tan with usually 9 dark saddle blotches on a green-brown mottled pattern; lateral region with 9–12 small, dark, rectangle-shaped blotches and 3 dark basicaudal spots; lower dorsal and ventral regions yellow to white with small, dark spots that may not be notable. The spines of the first dorsal fin are outlined in black with the other fins having faint brown bands. Breeding males have the above coloration in darker shades.

Slough darter, *Etheostoma gracile,* breeding adult, 2.1 in (53 mm)

Slough darter, *Etheostoma gracile,* nonbreeding adult, 1.9 in (48 mm)

Slough Darter

Etheostoma gracile (Girard, 1859)

RANGE: Nueces River basin north to the Red River basin.

HABITAT: Standing or slow-flowing water.

CHARACTERISTICS:

(1) Dark preorbital, postorbital, and suborbital bars; suborbital bars may be faint.

(2) Frenum present.

(3) Cheeks, opercles, and preopercles scaled; embedded scales may be present.

(4) Nape partly scaled to unscaled.

(5) Belly fully scaled; may be unscaled anteriorly.

(6) Dorsal region with mottled olive-brown pattern and 9–10 small, dark greenish brown saddle blotches that may be faint or absent.

(7) Males with 8–10 bright green vertical bars; may be absent on the lateral region.

Females with 8–10 dark green rectangular blotches; may be absent.

(8) Spots of pigmentation on breast and belly as well as pelvic fins of breeding males.

(9) First dorsal fin with 7–13 spines.

(10) Lateral line incomplete; lateral series scales: 40–55, with 13–27 pored. Lateral line appears as short stripe ending below first dorsal fin.

(11) Anal fin with 2 spines.

(12) Small, dark caudal spot.

DIMENSIONS: Up to 2.3 in (58 mm).

FIN COUNTS: Anal soft fin rays 5–8; dorsal soft fin rays 9–14; pectoral soft fin rays 12–14.

COLORATION: Head with dark preorbital, postorbital, and suborbital bars. Dorsal region mottled olive-brown with 8–10 dark green saddle blotches; lateral region light brown, with males usually having 8–10 bright green vertical bars and females usually having dark green rectangular blotches and a small, dark basicaudal spot; ventral region yellow or white.

Rio Grande darter,
Etheostoma grahami,
2 in (51 mm)

Rio Grande Darter

Etheostoma grahami (Girard, 1859)

RANGE: Rio Grande basin and lower portions of the Pecos River basin.

HABITAT: Rivers and creeks in riffles.

CHARACTERISTICS:

(1) Infraorbital and supraorbital canals interrupted.

(2) Preorbital bars notable.

(3) Cheeks with few scales.

(4) Opercles scaled.

(5) Breast unscaled.

(6) Belly scaled.

(7) Small, red dots on body that might form rows; black dots on females.

(8) Lateral region with 10–12 faint vertical bars; may not be notable.

(9) Lateral line incomplete; lateral series scales: 40–56, with 23–36 pored.

(10) First dorsal fin with 9–12 spines.

(11) Anal fin with 2 spines.

DIMENSIONS: Up to 2.3 in (58 mm).

FIN COUNTS: Anal soft fin rays 5–9; dorsal soft fin rays 10–13; pectoral soft fin rays 11–13.

COLORATION: Body with small red dots that might form rows; black dots on females. Dorsal region light green with 8–10 dark dorsal blotches; lateral region light green with faint vertical bars; ventral region yellow to white. Dorsal and pelvic fins on males are red, pectoral and caudal fins yellow with faint brown stripes. Dorsal and caudal fins of females have faint brown stripes; paired fins are clear. On breeding males, red fins and red spots become more intense in color.

COMMENTS: This species is listed by the state as threatened.

Harlequin darter, *Etheostoma histrio*, 2.8 in (71 mm)

Harlequin Darter

Etheostoma histrio Jordan and Gilbert, 1887

RANGE: Cypress, Sabine, Neches, and Trinity Rivers.
HABITAT: Rivers and creeks in runs.
CHARACTERISTICS:
(1) Frenum present; may be reduced or absent.
(2) Head short and round; head goes into standard body length 4.2 or more times.
(3) Branchiostegals broadly connected.
(4) Nape usually fully scaled.
(5) Belly, cheeks, and opercles unscaled to partly scaled.
(6) Breast unscaled.

(7) Lateral line scales: 45–58, with 0–3 unpored.
(8) Dark, green vertical bars (7–10) on lateral region.
(9) Pectoral fins longer than head.
(10) Base of caudal fin with 2 dark blotches.
(11) Anal fin with 2 spines.
DIMENSIONS: Up to 3 in (76 mm).
FIN COUNTS: Anal soft fin rays 6–8; dorsal soft fin rays 11–14; pectoral soft fin rays 13–16.
COLORATION: Dorsal region green with 6–7 dark brown dorsal saddles; lateral region green with 7–11 dark green or brown vertical bars; ventral region yellow green. Head, breast, second dorsal, caudal fin, and paired fins with dark brown or black spots. First dorsal fin with a red submarginal stripe and brown base; may have dark blotches anteriorly and posteriorly.

Greenthroat darter, *Etheostoma lepidum,* breeding adult, 2.3 in (58 mm)

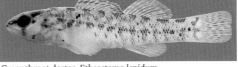

Greenthroat darter, *Etheostoma lepidum,* nonbreeding adult, 2 in (51 mm)

Greenthroat Darter

Etheostoma lepidum (Baird and Girard, 1853)

RANGE: Edwards Plateau region south to the Nueces River basin.

HABITAT: Headwaters, creeks, and rivers.

CHARACTERISTICS:

(1) Interrupted infraorbital and supratemporal canals

(2) Preorbital and suborbital bars.

(3) Nape partly scaled.

(4) Cheeks scaled to unscaled.

(5) Opercles unscaled.

(6) Breast unscaled to partly unscaled.

(7) Breast and branchiostegals green to blue-green, males only; females are white on these areas.

(8) Belly fully scaled; may be partly unscaled.

(9) Lateral region with 8–13 dark green bars; bars encircle body posteriorly.

(10) Lateral line incomplete; lateral series scales: 43–67, with 19–42 pored.

(11) First dorsal fin with 7–12 spines.

(12) Anal fin with 2 spines; may have 1 spine on rare occasions.

(13) Small, dark caudal spots (3) aligned vertically.

DIMENSIONS: Up to 2.5 in (64 mm).

FIN COUNTS: Anal soft fin rays 4–9; dorsal soft fin rays 8–14; pectoral soft fin rays 9–14.

COLORATION: Colors vary. Head with dark preorbital and suborbital bars; postorbital bars resemble dark spots. Dorsal region olive and may have dark saddle blotches; lateral region with 8–13 dark green–brown vertical bars; spaces between bars yellow flecked with orange; 3 small dark caudal spots aligned vertically; ventral region of males orange but white on females. Males have a first dorsal fin with blue-green margin, a clear submarginal stripe, and a broad red-orange base stripe; some may have blue-green base stripe. The second dorsal fin and caudal fin of males have red-brown spots in concentric stripes while the pelvic fins are a blue-green, sometimes with orange or red-orange medially. Females have fins with brown spots.

Goldstripe darter, *Etheostoma parvipinne*, 2.5 in (64 mm)

Goldstripe Darter

Etheostoma parvipinne Gilbert and Swain, 1887

RANGE: Brazos River basin northward and eastward to the Red River and Sabine River basin.

HABITAT: Headwaters and creeks in runs and pools.

CHARACTERISTICS:

(1) Snout short and blunt.

(2) Frenum present.

(3) Mouth small and upturned; prevomerine and palatine teeth present.

(4) Orbital bars notable.

(5) Nape fully scaled.

(6) Opercles fully scaled.

(7) Cheeks fully to partly scaled.

(8) Breast fully to partly scaled.

(9) Belly fully scaled.

(10) Branchiostegal membranes moderately to broadly joined.

(11) First dorsal fin with dark blotch anteriorly.

(12) Lateral region with mottled brown blotches (may resemble bars) bisected by a light golden lateral stripe. Stripe may be broken up by the lateral blotches; most notable in darters taken from vegetation.

(13) Lateral line incomplete; lateral series scales: 40–62, with 38–60 pored.

(14) Dorsal fin with 8–12 spines.

(15) Anal fin with 1–2 spines (usually 2).

(16) Up to 4 small, dark caudal spots aligned vertically.

DIMENSIONS: Up to 2.8 in (71 mm).

FIN COUNTS: Anal soft fin rays 7–10; dorsal soft fin rays 7–13; pectoral soft fin rays 13–17.

COLORATION: Head with dark orbital bars. Dorsal region light brown with up to 15 small, dark brown saddle blotches; lateral region with dark brown mottling, which may resemble bars, bisected by a light gold lateral stripe and dark caudal spots aligned vertically; ventral region white to yellow with small dark spots. First dorsal fin of males has dark blotch anteriorly.

Cypress darter, *Etheostoma proeliare,* breeding adult, 1.3 in (33 mm)

Cypress darter, *Etheostoma proeliare,* nonbreeding adult, 1.3 in (33 mm)

Cypress Darter

Etheostoma proeliare (Hay, 1881)

RANGE: San Jacinto River basin north to the Red River basin.

HABITAT: Standing or slow-flowing water.

CHARACTERISTICS:

(1) Orbital bars present.

(2) Interrupted supratemporal and infraorbital canals.

(3) Gill membranes moderately joined.

(4) Nape unscaled.

(5) Parietal region unscaled.

(6) Cheeks, opercles, and prepectoral area scaled.

(7) Belly unscaled to fully scaled; if partly scaled, scales on posterior portion of belly.

(8) Dorsal region with 6–9 dark brown saddle blotches; may be absent.

(9) Midlateral region with 7–12 dark brown dashes; may resemble blotches.

(10) First dorsal fin with 7–9 spines.

(11) Lateral line incomplete; lateral series scales: 34–38, with 0–9 pored.

(12) Anal fin with 2 spines.

DIMENSIONS: Up to 2 in (51 mm).

FIN COUNTS: Anal soft fin rays 4–7; dorsal soft fin rays 9–11.

COLORATION: Head with orbital bars. Dorsal region olive-brown with 7–12 dark brown saddle blotches; lateral region olive-brown with 6–9 midlateral dashes as well as dark spots forming a mottled pattern; ventral region white with scattered black spots. The first dorsal fin has a red median stripe while the second dorsal and caudal fin have brown stripes. Breeding males have darker colors and a first dorsal fin with a black base stripe and a medial row of red-orange spots. The second dorsal and caudal fins have orange stripes while anal and pelvic fins are black.

COMMENTS: The cypress darter can be distinguished from the fountain darter by its 2 anal fin spines versus 1 anal fin spine for the fountain darter and 8 dorsal fin spines versus 6, and occasionally 7, dorsal fin spines for the fountain darter.

Orangebelly darter, *Etheostoma radiosum,* male, 1.6 in (41 mm)

Orangebelly Darter

Etheostoma radiosum (Hubbs and Black, 1941)

RANGE: Red River basin.

HABITAT: Usually found in creeks and rivers with riffles.

CHARACTERISTICS:

(1) Dark orbital bars; large, dark humeral spots, posterior to opercles.

(2) Nape fully scaled.

(3) Cheek partly to fully scaled.

(4) Opercle unscaled to partly scaled.

(5) Belly fully scaled.

(6) Dorsal region with 8–10 dark saddle blotches.

(7) Lateral region with 8–12 dark blotches most notable below lateral line; lateral blotches on caudal peduncle form vertical bars (these bars connect to the saddle blotches on the caudal peduncle). It should also be noted that in some specimens the lateral region, not including the caudal peduncle, will have more of a mottled pattern.

(8) First dorsal fin with 9–12 spines.

(9) Lateral line incomplete; lateral series scales: 47–66, with 26–60 pored.

(10) Anal fin with 2 spines.

DIMENSIONS: Up to 3.5 in (85 cm).

FIN COUNTS: Anal soft fin rays 6–9; dorsal soft fin rays 11–17; pectoral soft fin rays 11–13.

COLORATION: Head with dark orbital bars and large dark humeral spot; dorsal region olive with 8–10 green saddle blotches; lateral region olive with dark green blotches or mottling that will form vertical bars on the caudal peduncle (dorsal saddle blotches connect to vertical bars on caudal peduncle); ventral region yellow-orange. Females have fins that are clear or yellow with blue margins on median fins. The first dorsal fin of females has an orange submarginal band and dark base band. In males, dorsal and caudal fins have blue margins and red-orange submarginal bands with a dark base band. The anal fin of males is red with a blue margin while the pelvic fins are yellow. Breeding males have the above colors in more intense tones as well as bright orange and blue-green bands in the median fins. The pelvic fins of breeding males are blue-green with orange tips while the pectoral fins are orange.

Orangethroat darter, *Etheostoma spectabile,* male, 1.6 in (41 mm)

Orangethroat darter, *Etheostoma spectabile,* female, 1.4 in (36 mm)

Orangethroat Darter
Etheostoma spectabile (Agassiz, 1854)

RANGE: San Antonio River basin north to the Red River basin.

HABITAT: Headwaters, creeks, and rivers in riffles, pools, and runs.

CHARACTERISTICS:

(1) Interrupted infraorbital canal.

(2) Orbital bars present.

(3) Frenum present.

(4) Nape unscaled to fully scaled.

(5) Cheeks and opercles unscaled to fully scaled.

(6) Branchiostegal membranes, throat, and, on occasion, breast bright orange; most notable on breeding males.

(7) Gill membranes separate to slightly joined.

(8) Breast unscaled; may have scales embedded posteriorly.

(9) Belly fully scaled.

(10) Dorsal region with 6–11 dark saddle blotches; may appear as mottled pattern.

(11) Upper portion of lateral region with dark spots forming short, horizontal stripes.

(12) Lateral region with 8–11 vertical bars; bars usually most distinct on lower portion.

(13) Lateral line incomplete; lateral series scales: 32–61, with 20–34 pored.

(14) First dorsal fin with 8–12 spines.

(15) Anal fin with 2 spines.

DIMENSIONS: Up to 2.7 in (69 mm).

FIN COUNTS: Anal soft fin rays 4–8; dorsal soft fin rays 10–15; pectoral soft fin rays 10–14.

COLORATION: Head with dark orbital bars. Dorsal region green to light olive with 6–11 dark saddle blotches; lateral region orange to pale yellow with 8–11 blue or brown vertical bars; ventral region yellow to white. Breeding males have bright orange branchiostegal membranes and throat.

Logperch, *Percina caprodes,* 5 in (127 mm)

Logperch

Percina caprodes (Rafinesque, 1818)

RANGE: Portions of the Red River drainage.

HABITAT: Rivers, creeks, and lakes.

CHARACTERISTICS:

(1) Suborbital bars present; may be faint.

(2) Snout pointed; may be conical and extend beyond lower lip on some specimens.

(3) Gill membranes separate; may be slightly joined.

(4) Opercles scaled.

(5) Cheeks scaled.

(6) Nape unscaled to partly scaled.

(7) Breast unscaled.

(8) Belly midline naked, females only; belly with row of 20–37 modified scales, males only.

(9) One to several modified scales between pelvic fins.

(10) Dorsal region with 15–20 brown vertical bars running onto lateral region, every other bar reaching to about the lateral line.

(11) Lateral line scales: 67–100, with 1–3 pored scales on caudal fin.

(12) Anal fin with 2 spines; in rare cases, 1 spine.

(13) Small, black caudal spot.

DIMENSIONS: Up to 7.3 in (185 mm).

FIN COUNTS: Anal soft fin rays 9–13; dorsal soft fin rays 14–18; pectoral soft fin rays 12–16.

COLORATION: Dorsal region brown to green; lateral region yellow with 15–20 brown vertical bars, with every other bar thin and reaching to about the lateral line; ventral region white to yellow.

COMMENTS: Several subspecies are known to exist in the United States and thus variation in the above characteristics might be encountered. This species is also known to hybridize with the blackside darter.

Texas logperch,
Percina carbonaria,
4.7 in (119 mm)

Texas Logperch

Percina carbonaria (Baird and Girard, 1853)

RANGE: Edwards Plateau region and northeastward to the Red River basin.

HABITAT: Rivers in riffles and runs.

CHARACTERISTICS:

(1) Dark suborbital bar.

(2) Nape covered with scales.

(3) Piglike snout.

(3) Supraoccipital region unscaled.

(4) Breast and prepectoral area unscaled.

(5) Cheeks and opercles scaled.

(6) Belly scaled, with a row of about 26–35 modified scales along the belly midline.

(7) Lateral line scales: 80–93, with 0–3 pored scales on caudal fin.

(8) Dorsal region with alternating short and long olive or brown vertical bars, shorter bars extending onto lateral region and longer bars onto ventral region. Bars are constricted, with center of bars thinner than top or bottom.

(9) Small, dark caudal spot.

DIMENSIONS: Up to 5.2 in (132 mm).

FIN COUNTS: Anal soft fin rays 9–11; dorsal soft fin rays 13–16; pectoral soft fin rays 12–15.

COLORATION: Head with dark suborbital bar; dorsal region light olive with alternating short and long olive or brown vertical bars, shorter bars extending onto lateral region and longer bars onto ventral region; lateral region light olive; ventral region cream colored. Breeding males have a black breast and black branchiostegal membranes, as well as black anal and pelvic fins; the first dorsal fin has a bright orange submarginal stripe.

COMMENTS: The Texas logperch can be distinguished from the bigscale logperch by its alternating long and short bars that are constricted versus 15–20 vertical bars of equal length on the bigscale logperch, and the suborbital bar versus lack of suborbital bar on the bigscale logperch.

Bigscale logperch,
*Percina macro-
lepida,* 4 in
(102 mm)

Bigscale Logperch

Percina macrolepida Stevenson, 1971

RANGE: Rio Grande basin northeast to the Red and Sabine river basins.

HABITAT: Impoundments as well as rivers in pools and runs.

CHARACTERISTICS:

(1) Suborbital bars; may be absent.

(2) Supraorbital region scaled.

(3) Nape scaled.

(4) Cheeks and opercles scaled.

(5) Prepectoral area scaled.

(6) Belly scaled, with a row of about 25 modified scales along belly midline. Bellies of males may be unscaled anteriorly, on females, unscaled along the midline of the body.

(7) Lateral line scales: 77–90, with 0–1 pored scales on caudal fin.

(8) Dorsal region with 15–20 dark green or black vertical bars running onto the lateral region, all bars about the same length.

(9) Small, dark caudal spot.

DIMENSIONS: Up to 4.2 in (107mm).

FIN COUNTS: Anal soft fin rays 7–10; dorsal soft fin rays 12–15.

COLORATION: Head with suborbital bars; dorsal region olive with 15–20 dark green or black vertical bars running onto the lateral region; lateral region olive with a dark caudal spot; ventral region cream colored with spots scattered over the venter. Caudal and dorsal fins with dark stripes; first dorsal fin has a tinge of yellow with remaining fins being mostly clear. Breeding males have shades of yellow or orange on the body with dusky anal and paired fins.

COMMENTS: The bigscale logperch can be distinguished from the Texas logperch by its 15–20 vertical bars of equal length versus the alternating long and short bars that are constricted on the Texas logperch and lack of a notable suborbital bar versus the notable suborbital bar on the Texas logperch.

Blackside darter,
Percina maculata,
3 in (76 mm)

Blackside Darter
Percina maculata (Girard)

RANGE: Northeastern portions of
the Red River basin.
HABITAT: Rivers and creeks in
pools.
CHARACTERISTICS:
(1) Suborbital bars present.
(2) Frenum present.
(3) Gill membranes barely connected
or separate.
(4) Opercles scaled.
(5) Cheeks scaled; may be only partly
scaled.
(6) Nape naked or with small embedded scales.
(7) Dark blotch at base of dorsal fin
between first and third spines.
(8) Lateral line scales: 53–81, none
pored.
(9) Lateral region with 6–9 black
blotches; may appear to be connected.
(10) Breast naked to partially scaled.
(11) Modified scales on breast and
posterior portion of belly.
(12) Anal fin with 2 spines.
(13) Small, dark caudal spot.
DIMENSIONS: Up to 4.5 in
(114 mm).
FIN COUNTS: Anal soft fin rays
7–13; dorsal soft fin rays 10–15; pectoral soft fin rays 11–16.
COLORATION: Dorsal region olive-
yellow to brown with mottling and
7–10 dark saddle blotches; lateral
region yellow to olive with 6–9 dark
blotches; ventral region yellowish to
white. Breeding males with the above
colors in darker shades; fins will be
dark.
COMMENTS: This species is listed
by the state as threatened.

Dusky darter,
Percina sciera,
4 in (102 mm)

Dusky Darter

Percina sciera (Swain, 1883)

RANGE: Guadalupe River basin
northeastward to the Red River basin.
HABITAT: Rivers and creeks in runs
and riffles.
CHARACTERISTICS:
(1) Frenum present.
(2) Nape scaled.
(3) Cheeks and opercles scaled.
(4) Suborbital bars absent or faint.
(5) Breast fully to partly scaled;
breast usually naked in females.
(6) Belly scaled; midline may be
naked on females, while males
have modified scales along body
midline.
(7) Gill membranes broadly joined.

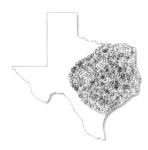

(8) First dorsal fin with dark blotch
posteriorly.
(9) Dorsal region with mottling and 8
small, dark saddle blotches, usually
indistinct.
(10) Lateral region with 8–12 black
blotches that may be connected.
(11) Caudal spots (3) aligned vertically, with lower 2 spots connected.
(12) Lateral line scales: 56–78.
(13) First dorsal fin with 11–14
spines.
(14) Anal fin with 2 spines.
DIMENSIONS: Up to 5 in
(127 mm).
FIN COUNTS: Anal soft fin rays
7–10; dorsal soft fin rays 11–13.
COLORATION: Dorsal region olive-green with mottling and 8 dark
saddle blotches; lateral region with
8–12 black, oval blotches, and 3 vertically aligned caudal spots of which
lower 2 are connected; ventral region
white. Breeding males become dark
and have black vertical bars extending over dorsal region.

Walleye, *Stizostedion vitreum,* 16 in (406 mm)

Walleye

Stizostedion vitreum (Mitchill, 1818)

RANGE: Introduced, walleye have been stocked in a number of reservoirs throughout the state.

HABITAT: Usually found in lakes and rivers with runs, pools, and backwaters.

CHARACTERISTICS:

(1) Eyes silvery and appear to glow in the dark.

(2) Mouth large and terminal; upper jaw reaches to about rear margin of eye.

(3) Canine teeth on premaxillaries, lower jaw, and roof of the mouth.

(4) Preopercle strongly serrate.

(5) Opercle scaled; cheeks with few or no scales.

(6) Nape scaled.

(7) Posterior portion of first dorsal fin with dark blotch.

(8) Second dorsal fin with dark spots in uniform rows.

(9) Dark pigmentation on base of pectoral fins.

(10) Dorsal region with 6–8 vague saddle blotches; may not be notable.

(11) Lateral line scales: 77–104.

(12) Anal fin with 2 spines.

(13) Caudal fin with rows of dark spots.

(14) Tip of anal fin and lower lobe of caudal fin white.

DIMENSIONS: Up to 36 in (914 mm).

FIN COUNTS: Anal soft fin rays 11–14; dorsal soft fin rays 18–22.

COLORATION: Dorsal region dark brown, olive, or yellow (may be mottled in coloration); lateral region greenish yellow with mottling; ventral region yellow to white. Posterior portion of first dorsal fin with black blotch; second dorsal fin has dark spots in uniform rows. Tip of anal fin and lower lobe of caudal fin are white. Juveniles possess 5–12 vague vertical bars on lateral region of the body.

COMMENTS: A young walleye differs from a young darter in that it has a strongly serrate preopercle and large mouth with the upper jaw reaching well past the pupil of the eye.

Freshwater drum, *Aplodinotus grunniens*, 7 in (178 mm)

Freshwater Drum

Aplodinotus grunniens Rafinesque, 1819

RANGE: Statewide, excluding the Panhandle and Trans-Pecos regions.

HABITAT: Lakes and rivers.

CHARACTERISTICS:

(1) Snout rounded.

(2) Canals of cephalic lateral line visible.

(3) Mouth subterminal.

(4) Dorsal region arched.

(5) First dorsal fin with 8–9 spines, second dorsal fin with 1 spine. Some publications note that this species has 2 dorsal fins connected by a membrane but only mention that the dorsal fin has 10 spines—the sum of the spines on the first and second dorsal fin.

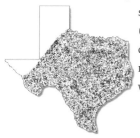

(6) Lateral line well developed and running onto caudal fin, with 48–53 scales.

(7) Pelvic fins with 1 spine; outer pelvic fin rays elongate.

(8) Anal fin with 2 spines, with second spine longer than the first.

(9) Caudal fin pointed.

DIMENSIONS: Up to 57 in (1448 mm) and 60 lbs (27 kg).

FIN COUNTS: Anal soft fin rays 7; dorsal soft fin rays 24–32; pelvic soft fin rays 5.

COLORATION: Dorsal region of body and head olive-brown to gray; lateral region silvery with specimens taken from clear water being a grayish white and turbid water specimens bronzy; ventral region white.

COMMENTS: By contraction of muscles along the walls of the air bladder, male freshwater drums can produce a sound described as drumming or humming (thought to attract females), thus the name "drum." The eggs and larvae of this species float at the surface of the water.

Banded pygmy sunfish, *Elassoma zonatum,* 0.5 in (13 mm)

Banded Pygmy Sunfish

Elassoma zonatum Jordan, 1877

RANGE: Brazos River basin north to the Red River basin.

HABITAT: Swamps, sloughs, and creeks.

CHARACTERISTICS:

(1) Mouth small and terminal.

(2) Dark spots (1 or 2) just below dorsal fin origin.

(3) Scales with melanophores, giving body a speckled pattern.

(4) Lateral region with 7–12 dark, vertical bars.

(5) Median fins with dark spots.

(6) Pectoral fins short and rounded; do not reach beyond eye when bent forward.

(7) Dorsal fin with 3–5 spines.

(8) Anal fin with 3 spines.

(9) Pelvic fins long and pointed, with 1 spine.

(10) Lateral line absent; 28–45 lateral series scales.

DIMENSIONS: Up to 1.7 in (43 mm).

FIN COUNTS: Anal soft fin rays 4–8; dorsal soft fin rays 8–13; pectoral soft fin rays 13–17; pelvic soft fin rays 5.

COLORATION: Entire body dark olive-green to brown with scale pigmentation giving body speckled appearance in addition to 7–12 dark, vertical bars. Dark spots (1 or 2) just below the dorsal fin origin; median fins with dark spots. Breeding males are almost solid black.

COMMENTS: The banded pygmy sunfish can be distinguished from a juvenile bass by its 3–5 dorsal spines.

Rio Grande cichlid, *Cichlasoma cyanoguttatum,* adult, 9 in (229 mm)

Rio Grande cichlid, *Cichlasoma cyanoguttatum,* juvenile, 1.2 in (30 mm)

Rio Grande Cichlid

Cichlasoma cyanoguttatum (Baird and Girard, 1854)

RANGE: Rio Grande and Pecos River basins. As a result of introductions this species can be also found in other areas of the state.

HABITAT: Lakes and rivers in pools and runs.

CHARACTERISTICS:

(1) Lateral region with 4–6 dark, vertical bars.

(2) Body with numerous small white spots.

(3) Dorsal fin with 15–17 spines.

(4) Anal fin with 5–7 spines.

(5) Iridescent blue-green spots (or wavy lines) on head, body, and fins, most notable on adults.

(6) Lateral region with 2 black spots; may be absent on adults.

(7) Interrupted lateral line.

DIMENSIONS: Up to 12 in (305 mm).

FIN COUNTS: Anal soft fin rays 9–10; dorsal soft fin rays 10–12.

COLORATION: Dorsal region dark olive; lateral region blue-green with 2 dark midlateral blotches. Body and fins covered with small white to blue spots in addition to larger iridescent blue-green spots (or wavy lines). Breeding Rio Grande cichlids are white on anterior half of body and black on posterior half of body.

COMMENTS: The Rio Grande cichlid is the only cichlid native to the United States.

Blue tilapia, *Oreochromis aurea,* adult, 9.4 in (239 mm)

Blue tilapia, *Oreochromis aurea,* juvenile, 1.5 in (38 mm)

Blue Tilapia
Oreochromis aurea (Stiendachner, 1864)

RANGE: Rio Grande, Guadalupe River, and Colorado River basins. Found in other areas of the state as a result of introductions.

HABITAT: Usually found in warm water of ponds and impoundments. The blue tilapia is intolerant of cold water and restricted to warm regions or impoundments heated by power plant effluent or warm springs.

CHARACTERISTICS:

(1) Mouth moderate in size and terminal.

(2) Outer row of teeth bicuspid; most notable in adults.

(3) Dorsal fin with red margin.

(4) Interrupted lateral line.

(5) Anal fin with 3 spines.

(6) Posterior margin of caudal fin red.

DIMENSIONS: Up to 17.5 in (445 mm) and 4.2 lbs (1.9 kg).

FIN COUNTS: Dorsal soft fin rays 12–15.

COLORATION: Dorsal and lateral regions silver-gray with dorsal and caudal fins having red margins. Breeding males have a bright, metallic blue head with a dark blue to black chin and breast with the remainder of the body pale blue. Juveniles have vertical bars on the body and caudal fin.

Appendix

Counting Pharyngeal Teeth

Pharyngeal teeth appear as toothlike projections protruding from the fifth pair of bony gill arches (also termed pharyngeal arches) embedded just posterior to the gill-bearing arches.

Pharyngeal arch

Each arch will typically have one or two rows of teeth or, in the case of the common carp (*Cyprinus carpio*), three rows. The function of these teeth varies among species, from holding prey in the mouth to ripping, mashing, or grinding food items. The shape of the teeth usually gives an indication of their purpose (e.g., clawlike teeth are for ripping and tearing; molarlike teeth are for mashing and grinding).

Counts of pharyngeal teeth can serve as a means of identifying some fishes of the family Cyprinidae. The formula for counting these teeth is as follows: count from the left arch, with the inner row (or lesser row) being counted first, followed by the outer row (or main row). One then moves to the right arch and counts the teeth in the outer row and concludes with the inner row.

Thus, in the example for family Cyprinidae the pharyngeal tooth formula would be written as 1,4–4,2. However, the number of teeth in each row is not

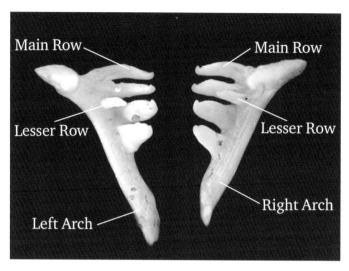

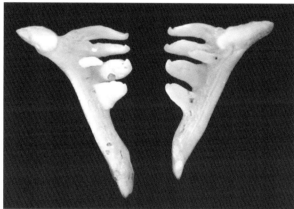

Dorsal view of pharyngeal teeth of minnow spp., with arches rotated outward so teeth are visible

always uniform (e.g., 2,4-4,1), and you might see differences in either the main rows or lesser rows (e.g., 2,5-4,2 or 2,4-4,1). The common carp (*Cyprinus carpio*) has three rows of teeth to contend with, but the rules still apply: left arch (inner, middle, and outer portion) and then the right arch (outer, middle, and inner portion). The resulting count of pharyngeal teeth would be written as 1,1,3-3,1,1.

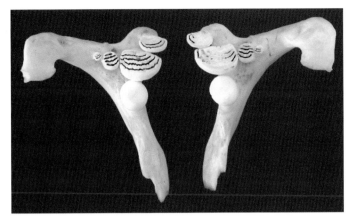

Dorsal view of pharyngeal teeth of common carp, with arches rotated outward so teeth are visible

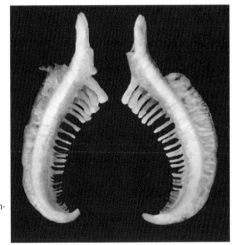

Dorsal view of pharyngeal teeth of sucker spp.

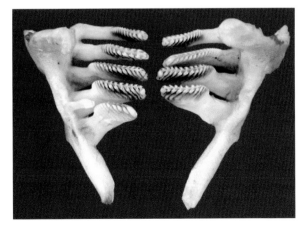

Dorsal view of pharyngeal teeth of grass carp, with arches rotated outward so teeth are visible

Glossary

adipose eyelid.   Fleshy tissue around the edge of the eye (outlined by dotted lines), present only on a few species, such as shad and mullet (Fig. A).

adipose fin.   Fleshy rayless fin on the middle of the back between the dorsal and the caudal fin (Fig. B).

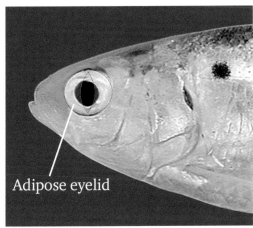

Adipose eyelid

Fig. A

Dorsal fin   Adipose fin

Barbels   Anal fin

Fig. B

anal fin.   Ventral unpaired fin (see Fig. B).

anterior.   Refers to being in front of, as in "the base of the first dorsal fin is anterior to the base of the second dorsal fin" (Fig. C).

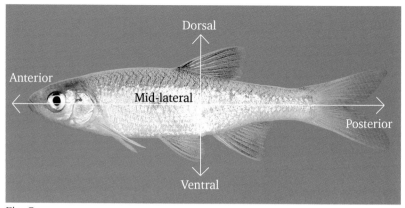

Fig. C

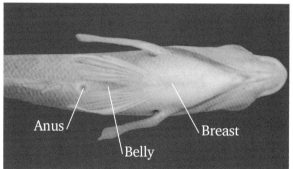

Fig. D

anus.   External opening for the digestive system (Fig. D).

axillary scale.   An enlarged, extending scale associated with the paired fins in some fishes, such as shads and mullets (Fig. E).

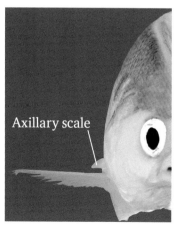

Fig. E

barbels. Slender, flexible, fleshy processes located near the mouth and functioning as sensors for taste and touch (see Fig. B).

belly. Ventral surface of the abdominal region (see Fig. D).

bound gill membranes. Membrane attached to isthmus; a probe tip slipped underneath gill cleft will not freely pass to other gill cleft (Fig. F).

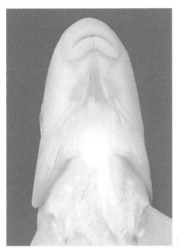 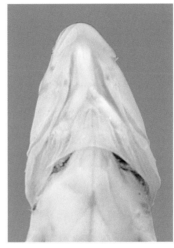

Fig. F   Fig. G

breast. Ventral surface of the body anterior to the belly (see Fig. D).

broadly joined gill membranes. Membranes joined (not attached) across isthmus, with isthmus being almost entirely covered (Fig. G).

canine. Tall, sharp teeth set in one or two rows (Fig. H).

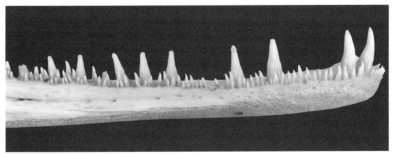

Fig. H

caudal fin.   The tail fin (Fig. I), which may be either forked (Fig. Ia), rounded
(Fig. Ib), truncate (Fig. Ic), pointed (Fig. Id), or emarginate (Fig. Ie).

caudal peduncle.   Narrow region of the body in front of the caudal fin (see
Fig. I).

Fig. I

Fig. Ia

Fig. Ib

Fig. Ic

Fig. Id

Fig. Ie

cheek.   The area between the eye and preopercle bone (see Fig. I).

ctenoid scales.   Type of scales found on most spiny ray fishes (Fig. J).

cycloid scales.   Type of scales of most soft ray fishes (Fig. K).

Fig. J

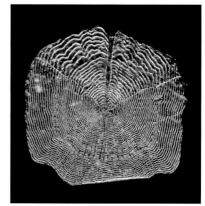

Fig. K

dorsal.   Refers to the top region or the back of a fish (see Fig. C).

dorsal fin.   Median unpaired fin(s) on the back, not including the adipose fin (see Fig. B).

fin insertion.   Anterior end of the bases of the paired fins (see Fig. I).

fin origin.   The anterior end of a fin base (see Fig. I).

first dorsal fin.   The anterior fin when two fins are present (Fig. L).

frenum.   Ridge or fold of tissue that binds the upper jaw to the snout (Fig. M).

First dorsal fin   Second dorsal fin

Fig. L

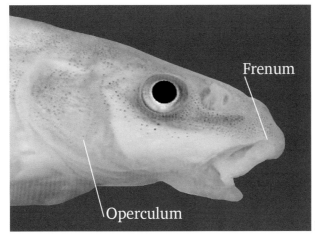

Frenum

Operculum

Fig. M

Fig. N

ganoid scales. Type of scales found covering the gars (Fig. N).

gill arch. Bones that support the gill filaments and rakers (Fig. O).

gill filaments. Respiratory structures projecting posteriorly from the gill arches (see Fig. O).

gill rakers. Hard projections from the concave anterior surface of the gill arches (see Fig. O).

gonopodium. Modified anal fin of the male of some species used to transfer sperm to the female genital pore (Fig. P).

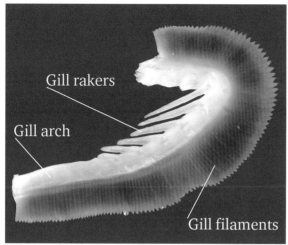

Gill rakers

Gill arch

Gill filaments Fig. O

Gonopodium

Fig. P

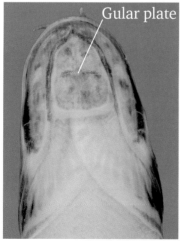

Gular plate

Fig. Q

Fig. R   Fig. S

gular plate.   Large median dermal bone on the throat (Fig. Q).

incisors.   Cutting teeth (Fig. R).

inferior.   Mouth that opens downward and is overhung by snout (Fig. S).

isthmus.   Part of the breast that projects forward between the gill chambers (Fig. T).

lateral line.   Part of the lateral line system, with cephalic lateral line canals (Fig. U).

mandible.   Lower jaw (Fig. V).

maxillary.   Bone of each upper jaw that lies immediately above or behind and parallel to the premaxillary (see Fig. V).

midlateral.   Refers to the midsides of a fish (see Fig. C).

moderately/slightly joined gill membranes.   Membranes joined across, not attached to isthmus, with isthmus only slightly covered (Fig. W).

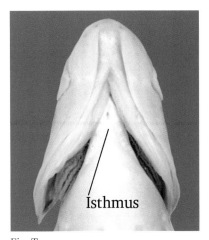

Fig. T

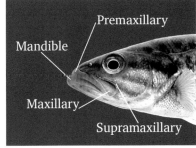

Fig. V

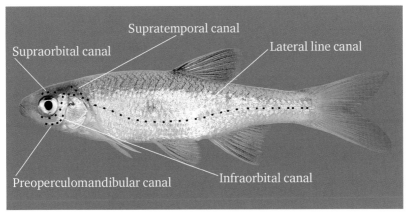

Fig. U

Fig. W

molariform.   Grinding teeth (Fig. X).

nape.   Dorsal part of the body from the occiput to the origin of the dorsal fin (Fig. Y).

occiput.   The posterior dorsal end of the head, often marked by a line separating scaled and scaleless portions of skin, where the head joins the dorsal mass (see Fig. Y).

operculum.   Flaps covering the gill chamber (see Fig. M).

pectoral fins.   Paired fins on the side, or on the breast, behind the head and associated with the pelvic girdle (see Fig. Z).

pelvic fins.   Ventral, paired fins associated with the pelvic girdle (Fig. Z).

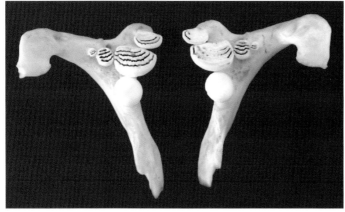

Fig. X

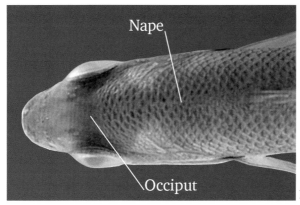

Fig. Y

posterior.   Refers to being located behind some structure or area (see Fig. C).

pseudobranchium.   Accessory gill on the inside surface of the operculum (Fig. AA).

premaxillary.   Paired bone at the front of the upper jaw (see Fig. V).

scutes.   Row of raised scales along the ventral portion of the body; most notable on shads (Fig. BB).

second dorsal fin.   The posterior fin when two dorsal fins are present (see Fig. L).

separate gill membranes.   Membranes separate, not joined to each other or to the isthmus (Fig. CC).

snout.   Part of the head anterior to the eye and not including the upper jaw (see Fig. I).

Pectoral fin/   \Pelvic fin

Fig. Z

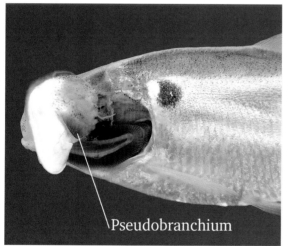

\Pseudobranchium

Fig. AA

soft ray. A soft, segmented, biserial (equal right and left halves) fin support that is usually branched (Fig. DD).

spine. A sharp, hard, uniserial fin support that is neither branched nor segmented and may be flexible on some fishes (Fig. EE).

subterminal. Slightly overhung by snout; opens horizontally (Fig. FF).

superior. Opens at top of head (Fig. GG).

terminal oblique. Opens at anterior of head with mouth opening slanting upward (Fig. HH).

terminal horizontal. Opens at anterior of head with mouth opening horizontal (Fig. II).

ventral. Refers to bottom or underside of a fish (see Fig. C).

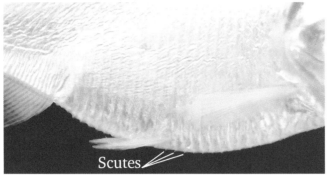

Fig. BB

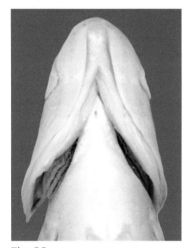

Fig. CC

Fig. DD

Fig. EE

Fig. GG

Fig. FF

Fig. HH   Fig. II

References

Becker, G. C. 1983. *Fishes of Wisconsin.* Madison: University of Wisconsin Press.

Blair, F. W., A. P. Blair, P. Brodkorb, F. R. Cagle, and G. A. Moore. 1957. *Vertebrates of the United States.* New York: McGraw-Hill.

Bond, C. E. 1996. *Biology of fishes.* 2nd ed. Fort Worth, Tex.: Saunders College Publishing.

Clay, W. M. 1975. *The fishes of Kentucky.* Frankfort: Kentucky Department of Fish and Wildlife Resources.

Cross, F. B., and J. T. Collins. 1975. *Fishes in Kansas.* Lawrence: University of Kansas.

Douglas, N. H. 1974. *Freshwater fishes of Louisiana.* Baton Rouge, La.: Claitor's Publishing Division.

Eddy, S. 1957. *How to know the freshwater fishes.* Dubuque, Iowa: William C. Brown Company.

Eisenhour, D. J. 2004. Systematics, variation, and speciation of the *Macrhybopsis aestivalis* complex west of the Mississippi River. *Bulletin of the Alabama Museum of Natural History* 23:9–48.

Etnier, D. A., and W. C. Starnes. 1993. *The fishes of Tennessee.* Knoxville: University of Tennessee Press.

Hendrickson, D. 1998–2004. Texas Natural History Collections: Ichthyology. Texas Memorial Museum, University of Texas at Austin. http://www.utexas .edu/tmm/tnhc/fish/.

Hubbs, C., R. J. Edwards, and G. P. Garrett. 1991. An annotated checklist of the freshwater fishes of Texas, with keys to identification of species. *Texas Journal of Science,* supplement, 43:1–56.

Hubbs, C., and K. Lagler. 1949. *Fishes of the Great Lakes region.* Ann Arbor: University of Michigan Press.

Kelsch, S. W., and F. S. Hendricks. 1986. An electrophoretic and multivariate comparison of the American catfishes *I. lupus* and *I. punctatus. Copeia* 1986:646–52.

———. 1990. Distribution of the headwater catfish *Ictalurus lupus* (Osteichthyes: Ictaluridae). *Southwestern Naturalist* 35:292–97.

Kent, G. C., and R. K. Carr. 2001. *Comparative anatomy of the vertebrates.* 9th ed. Boston: McGraw-Hill.

Miller, R. J., and H. W. Robison. 1973. *The fishes of Oklahoma.* Stillwater: Oklahoma State University Press.

Moyle, P. B., and J. J. Cech Jr. 2000. *Fishes: an introduction to ichthyology.* 4th ed. Upper Saddle River, N.J.: Prentice Hall.

Nelson, J. S., E. J. Crossman, H. Espinosa-Pérez, L. T. Findley, C. R. Gilbert, R. N. Lea, and J. D. Williams. 2004. *Common and scientific names of fishes from the United States, Canada, and Mexico.* 6th ed. Bethesda, Md.: American Fisheries Society Special Publication 29.

Page, L. M. 1983. *Handbook of darters.* Neptune City, N.J.: TFH Publications.

Pflieger, W. L. 1975. *The fishes of Missouri.* Jefferson City: Missouri Department of Conservation.

Phillips, G. L., W. D. Schmid, and J. C. Underhill. 1982. *Freshwater fishes of Minnesota.* Minneapolis: University of Minnesota Press.

Robison, H. W., and T. M. Buchanan. 1988. *The fishes of Arkansas.* Fayetteville: University of Arkansas Press.

Ross, S. T., W. M. Brenneman, W. T. Slack, M. T. O'Connell, and T. L. Peterson. 2001. *The inland fishes of Mississippi.* Jackson: University Press of Mississippi.

Smith, W. S. 1979. *The fishes of Illinois.* Urbana: Published for the Illinois State Natural History Survey by the University of Illinois Press.

Texas Parks and Wildlife Department. 2005. Endangered and threatened fish in Texas and the United States. http://www.tpwd.state.tx.us/huntwild/wild/species/endang/animals/fish/.

Trautman, M. B. 1957. *The fishes of Ohio with illustrated keys.* Rev. ed. Columbus: Ohio State University Press, in collaboration with the Ohio Division of Wildlife and the Ohio State University Development Fund.

Underwood, D. M., A. A. Echelle, D. J. Eisenhour, M. D. Jones, A. F. Echelle, and W. L. Fisher. 2003. Genetic variation in western members of the *Macrhybopsis aestivalis* complex (Telcostei. Cyprinidae), with emphasis on those of the Red and Arkansas river basins. *Copeia* 2003:493–501.

Index